"If the last few years have stolen your joy, this book will bring it back, 10-fold. What I love about *Joy-Full AF* is that Dr. Erin Burgoon first defines, makes the case for, and then shows us how to uncover the Joy in our lives. Using their own journey and numerous case studies, they anticipate our arguments and resistance, making the goal all the more attainable."

~ Mark J. Silverman,
author of the bestselling *Only 10s 2.0*
and host of the *Mastering Overwhelm* podcast

"*Joy-Full AF* is inspiring AF. As a corporate refugee who initially created a business that filled my bank account but drained my soul, I couldn't agree more that putting joy front and center is a life-changing approach. Erin shares brilliant questions and concepts that'll inspire you to create *your* unique journey to joy-full. I still wear my HILA hat every day. I guarantee you're going to want one, too…"

~ Shelley Paxton,
author of *Soulbbatical: A Corporate Rebel's Guide to Finding Your Best Life*

" This book will prove to be a road map, a wake-up call, or a lifesaver for you. Maybe all 3. Erin is one of the most authentic people I've ever known, fully committed to living a passionate life and advocating for others to do the same. This book is literally an actionable strategy guide for increasing the level of joy in your life, which is actually the main thing we all care about.
It's broken down into real-life consumable and digestible bits. The 4 ingredients of Joy shifted my consciousness immediately, and it only got better from there. If you act upon the wisdom inside, your life will be forever changed. **"**

~ Sean Smith,
speaker, coach, author, poet, actor,
founder of Neuro-Transformational Coaching

" In *Joy-Full AF*, Dr. Erin Burgoon deftly presents a compelling case for the inclusion of joy in all areas of business. This message that joy is a strategy for success in business is long overdue! The clarity provided around *"Be careful not to chase happiness at the expense of your joy"* alone can 10x your joy level immediately. They have done a fantastic job of taking something as intrinsic as joy that, up until now, has been rather cryptic in the business world, and made it accessible and actionable to everyone. *Joy-Full AF* is your roadmap to having success chase you. **"**

~ Ken Bechtel,
author of *Follow Your YES*

❝ Dr. Erin Burgoon has a PhD in psychology and a career background as a high-level leader in the world of technology. A coach and consultant to executives and entrepreneurs, Erin is helping leaders bring joy back to their lives and their careers. Let's be honest, all the success, money and recognition you have is meaningless if you're not happy. *Joy-Full AF* will help you see that joy is not just a result, it's the path to your next level of success. ❞

~ Rich Litvin,
founder of 4PC and coauthor of *The Prosperous Coach*

❝ Joy is not a frivolous nice-to-have. It's the way that smart leaders avoid creative and physical burnout. Erin's words are a compass for the "meh" that so many leaders are feeling. *Joy-Full AF* is fast-paced, wise, and full of aha moments you'll scribble onto sticky notes. This book feels like a chat with that really smart friend, who always helps you to see what's truly important. Provocative and clever, Erin's words will help you to swap "shoulds" and "supposed tos" for a daily dose of joy. ❞

~ Dr. Mandy Lehto,
host of *Enough, the podcast*

> In *Joy-Full AF*, Dr. Erin Burgoon takes us on a journey to pull apart joy, discover what it truly is, and from that true place finally allow ourselves to experience more of it. It's about time someone looked at joy as a measure of success in the same way hope is a measure of how fully you've released an old paradigm. This book will help you befriend joy without making the lack of it fuel for shame—a game-changer for business owners!

~ Catherine Hammond,
Life Transition Guide, award-winning attorney,
and author of *Hope(less)*

> Joy is a vital part of what makes us human. In this book, that is written with care, energy and heart, Dr. Erin Burgoon shares with us their insights into how you can have more joy in work and life. Allow your skeptical selves to revel in the wonderful world of Joy. Trust me when I say it—you will not regret it.

~ Em Stroud,
clown, author, podcaster and cofounder of Laugh.Think.Play.

❝ Dr. Erin Burgoon has written an amazing book that feels like a series of conversations with a new friend who prioritizes your well-being. *Joy-Full AF* made me realize how little I know about joy and then taught me how to cultivate it. Most importantly, its pages empowered me to recognize joy when it shows up in my life and business journeys. This book is a game changer. ❞

~ Addison Brasil,
author of the bestselling *The First Year of Grief Club*

❝ Thank you, Dr. Erin Burgoon, for writing the definitive book on one of the world's most ambiguously defined emotions. *Joy-Full AF* is a delightful and, importantly, *actionable* treatise on joy. Burgoon deftly explains what joy is and isn't, and shows us how we can find more of it in business and in our everyday lives. A scientist by background, Burgoon takes joy down to the studs and keenly examines its parts — connection, curiosity, creativity, and courage — before ultimately rebuilding it into something we can all embody and experience regularly. (INSERT HUGE SIGH OF RELIEF!) *Joy-Full AF* has inspired me to lead with joy instead of thinking of it like some kind of nice-to-have accessory. Now I see it for what it is: essential. ❞

~ Laurie Shiers,
Creativity Catalyst

“ No lie—I quoted several things I read in this book the day after reading the first half of it! HILA and magic beans immediately gave me a new, game-changing perspective. And there is one question Erin Burgoon mentions in the book that energized me to rethink so much about the direction I take my business in. Every entrepreneur needs to read this book (or every aspiring entrepreneur)! In this age of a million gurus teaching you the exact steps or right path, we've all lost sight of the fact that if we do what brings us the most joy, we'll inherently do it better and with more success. ”

~ Erin Hatzikostas,
Founder & CEO, b Authentic inc,
and author of *You Do You(ish)*

Joy-Full AF

Joy-Full AF

**THE ESSENTIAL BUSINESS STRATEGY
WE'RE AFRAID TO PUT FIRST**

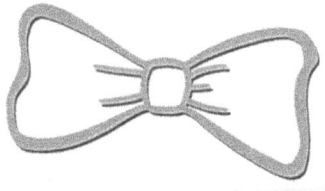

ERIN BURGOON, PhD

Joy-Full AF

Copyright © 2022-2025 by Erin Burgoon, PhD. All rights reserved. No part of this publication may be reproduced or transmitted in any form or by any means, mechanical or electronic, including photocopying and recording, or by any information storage and retrieval systems, without permission in writing from the author or publisher.

Disclaimer: The advice and strategies contained herein may not be suitable for every situation. This work is sold with the understanding that the Author and Publisher are not engaged in rendering legal, accounting, or other professional services. Neither the Author nor the Publisher shall be liable for damages arising herefrom. The fact that an organization or website is referred to in this work as a citation or a potential source of further information does not mean that the Author or the Publisher endorses the information that the organization or website may provide or recommendations it may make.

Book Design: Dino Marino Design, www.dinomarinodesign.com

Paperback ISBN - 979-8-9866335-3-4

Hardcover ISBN - 979-8-9866335-4-1

eBook ISBN - 979-8-9866335-5-8

DEDICATION

To my clients past, current, and future.
Your commitment to finding and following your joy,
and really, finding and following ***you***
inspires me beyond words.

Table of Contents

FOREWORD
    by Simone Seol, Joyful Marketing Coach............................. i

INTRODUCTION .... **IV**
    Why Did I Write a Book on Joy-Full AF Business?............. iv
    What's the Most Joy-full Way to Read *Joy-Full AF*? x

WHAT THE F*CK IS JOY ANYWAY? **1**
    What the F*ck is Joy Anyway? 3
    The Four Foundational Ingredients of Joy 7
    The Four Ingredients: Connection 10
    The Four Ingredients: Curiosity 14
    Why is Curiosity So F*cking Hard? 17
    The Four Ingredients: Creativity 22
    The Four Ingredients: Courage 24
    Taste the Rainbow 27
    I Sought Joy; I Found Me 29
    Joy-full AF, Not Joyful AF 32

WHY THE F*CK DO WE NEED JOY? **35**
    Why the F*ck Do We Need Joy? 37
    Misery Isn't Sustainable 39
    But Joy Is 42
    It's the Way Out of the Matrix 44

WHY ARE WE AFRAID TO PUT JOY FIRST? 47

Why Are We Afraid to Put Joy First? 49
Listen All Y'all, It's a Sabotage 51
Joy is Uncomfortable 55
Zebra Cakes, Reality TV, and Joy 58
For Joy or Money? 60

THE JOY AUDIT 63

HOW THE F*CK DO WE LOSE JOY (AND HOW CAN WE GET IT BACK?) 67

How The F*ck Do We Lose Joy
(And How Can We Get it Back?) 69
Stopping Yourself Before You Get Started 72
Tell Me Why (Ain't Nothing But a Heartache)...74
We Don't Need No Destination! 77
How Do I 81
Who Do I Need to Be? 84
"Just Follow My 10-Step Blueprint!" 86
I Will Teach You to Be Rich 89
Look Around, Look Around ...
At What Others Are Doing Right Now 93
Comparison is a Thief of Joy ... or Maybe Not ...96
Consistency is *Also* the Thief of Joy 102
The Unwritten Rules 106
Shoulding On Yourself 112
Are Your Goals Stealing Your Joy? 116
"How Monsters", Inner Critics,
and the Killjoys of Long-Term Goals 117

Goal Trap #1 - Heading Toward Destinations
on Other People's Maps..121
Goal Trap #2 - Going After Possible Goals........................123
Goal Trap #3 - Chasing Happiness 125
Goal Trap #4 - Chasing Enoughness 127
Falling Into Multiple Traps at Once...................................129
More More More 134
Hello, It's Me, Your Nervous System.................................136
When Your Body Says No, But You Still Go Go Go..........138
Going To Battle Against Your Nervous System 141
Uncomfortable Versus Unsafe...146
Focus on the Present ... But Not *Too* Much 150
Cutting Off, Exiling, or Stuffing Down "Parts" of You
That "Don't Belong in Business" 153
~~Love~~ Joy and Basketball..157

HOW THE F*CK DO WE GET MORE JOY?.. 165

How The F*ck Do We Get More Joy?................................167
... AND it's Joy-Full (Baking Joy into Every Goal) 170
When Do You Feel Joy-full? 173
What Makes You Come Alive?...176
Finding the *Most* Joy-full Path 179
Create Metrics for ~~Success~~ Joy 185
Want More Joy? Feel Your Pain..190
There is No Joy Without Rest...192
What is This, Amateur Hour?
(the Joy of Being a Newbie)..195
You Can't Imagine Yet What's Over the Horizon..............202

Fe-Fi-Fo-Fum ... Plant Some Magic Beans 206

Put on Your HILA Hat..211

It's All Fun and Games ...
No, Really!..217

"It's All Research" 226

Data Hath No Meaning 228

Joy Guides;
Experiment Decides 234

It's An 'Experiment' 239

Put on Your Lab Coat
AND Feel Your Feelings Too 242

Never Hike in The Business Wilderness Alone 245

Frodo and His Merry Band
of Travelers 247

Running Buddies 251

Keep Your Joy Tank Topped Off 255

EPILOGUE:
What Happens If We All Follow Our Joy? 259

RESOURCES... **263**

ACKNOWLEDGMENTS **266**

ABOUT THE AUTHOR **269**

Foreword

by Simone Seol

Let me ask you a question. Which path to happiness were you sold?

When I was a kid, I was taught that, if I studied hard, listened to what my parents and teachers said, and got into a good college, I'd be happy.

So I did that. And I wasn't happy. In fact, I was a tight ball of anxiety.

When I was in college, I was taught that, if I worked hard and put myself on a respectable career trajectory, I'd be happy.

So I did that. And I wasn't happy. In fact, I felt so lost and confused.

When I started my own business, I started repeating the same dynamic. If I follow the right directions, have the right mindset, get the good 'grades' (which, in entrepreneurship, meant money), I'd be happy.

The happiness never came. Neither did the money. In fact, all I got was burnout.

It wasn't until I figured out how to prioritize one secret, subversive ingredient that my business actually started to work, and make me money.

And you guessed it. That ingredient was joy.

The best part of it was, when I started using joy as a compass and barometer for every aspect of business planning, I didn't have to wait until I made more money to feel good.

I remember a particular moment of realizing: "This is it. I made it." It wasn't because of any flashy, impressive milestone I achieved. It was because I actually enjoyed being alive. I liked being myself. I enjoyed my business. That sense of being at home in my own life and pursuits was what I had actually been working toward my whole life, although I didn't know it.

No amount of money or external success could give it to me. Centering joy was what gave it to me.

Since then, I've become a champion of joy in my own way.

That is all to say, Erin and I share a subversive mission. To save other entrepreneurs the years of trial and error we both went through, and set them on the fastest possible path toward a joyful business. We also want to emphatically convey that joy isn't a childish, silly, or "nice to have" extra that you give yourself when you have time for a vacation.

It's essential to you, your customer base, and the world.

It's essential to your creativity, and even your health.

You don't have to try a million other things first, and accidentally stumble on joy as the last stop. You can just skip straight to it, and reap the rewards. And fortunately for us, we have in our hands this friendly, down-to-earth and deeply wise guide of a book to walk you every step of the way.

To be sure, Erin isn't the only person talking about joy. But they may be the only person who answers the gnarly, unspoken questions that few dare to tackle head on:

1. What exactly is joy, anyway?
2. Why can it feel so hard and elusive to find sometimes?
3. And how exactly does one go about creating it?

FOREWORD

In answering these questions, Erin clarifies and concretizes what may have felt abstract and nebulous. The four foundational ingredients of joy, introduced in this book, are a revolutionary anchor that enables you to create joy on purpose in any area of life, and in every context.

The greatest gift of this book is that it makes joy actionable and pragmatic. By the time you're done reading it, you might just be feeling a ton of it — even when looking at your business plan.

–Simone Seol is a Joyful Marketing Coach, host of *Joyful Marketing* podcast, and author of *The Fearless Marketing Bible for Coaches*

Introduction

WHY DID I WRITE A BOOK ON JOY-FULL AF BUSINESS?

To be honest, that wasn't the plan.

When I first committed to writing a book, I wanted to write about the power of my favorite word in the English language: And.

At the time, I had done almost thirty episodes of a podcast called *Life in the And*. My guests and small community of listeners were resonating with the concept, so I figured I could reach even more people if I expanded it into a book.

One of my podcast guests was my friend, Niiamah Ashong. He didn't talk about it on the show, but for years he had been contemplating creating a movement called The World Joy Movement. It was perfect for him. Niiamah is an extrovert with an infectious energy and a smile that stretches well beyond his face. He epitomizes joy and joy-fullness. Yet, whenever he talked about his movement, it didn't land for me. Joy wasn't on my radar. It wasn't even in my vocabulary. And I certainly didn't see it as having any relevance to business.

Not long after I hired a book coach to bring my "And" concept to life I realized "Life in the And" as a podcast, and as a potential book, were limiting what I wanted to share. I had so much more to offer that was getting buried.

And quite frankly, I was getting bored.

This was the first of many times in my book-writing process that I lost the joy. (Though I couldn't have articulated that's what was happening back then.) So, I decided to take a step back from writing.

One day, I pulled out a piece of paper and my colored pencils and wrote out a timeline of how my business developed beginning in April 2018.

In green, I listed my successes. The first clients I enrolled several months before I left the corporate world. The day my first group coaching program started. The day I raised my fees far beyond what I thought I would ever make as a coach.

In red, I wrote my failures. When I tried to launch a group, and no one enrolled. When I had a long and painful string of people say no to working with me. Going through a multiple-month dry spell of zero revenue when I thought seriously about giving up entirely on having a private coaching practice.

In blue, I wrote some of the activities that I did in those two years. The time I played the 90-day money game (which we'll talk about in *It's All Fun and Games … No, Really!*). When I joined one of the communities of coaches — 4PC — that really spurred my growth. Starting a 90-day live challenge on Facebook. Launching and later sunsetting my Facebook community, "The Heart Leader Launchpad."

In pink, I wrote the insights and thoughts I was having at that moment, like how I learned to continue showing up day after day, even during that dry spell when it felt like I was banging my head against the wall.

INTRODUCTION

I realized through the exercise that I had all kinds of things to share about how to have fun, play, step into courage, and move through fear.

But it still didn't occur to me that it was all about joy.

Joy was not in my vocabulary yet. Instead, the colored-pencil exercise sparked an idea for a book called *The 10 Essentials*, set in the business wilderness. After all, aren't we all on an adventure of bushwhacking, climbing mountains, and getting lost? When you go into the real wilderness, you always want to bring supplies for fire, food, water, and extra shelter — The Essentials. I wondered which "essentials" were pivotal to me thriving in business.

I looked back at my colored-pencil timeline and saw several concepts and tools that could be represented by objects. I *love* to experiment. So, I saw a lab coat. One of my favorite concepts in goal setting is High Intentions and Low Attachment or HILA. I thought of it as a hat you put on. Feeling like I had traction with *The 10 Essentials*, I feverishly wrote chapters, confident that I was naming powerful teaching tools and also creating a fun metaphor to teach them through. But I had an underlying nagging feeling that something was missing. I had already written half the book by the time I noticed that despite having one of the most fun and playful concepts for a book that I could imagine, I wasn't having fun or feeling playful. (I'd lost the joy, but I *still* didn't have that word in my vocabulary.)

I procrastinated. I made excuses to do other things. I felt exhausted every time I sat down to write.

When I took a month off from my business in the summer to write and recharge, I only opened Microsoft Word once. I thought, at the time, that maybe I just really needed a vacation and that I'd pick the book back up after.

When I came back, I still didn't want to open Word. I considered many options and it ultimately seemed like the only solution was to shelve the book. Maybe I just wasn't meant to write a book after all.

But the concepts kept coming back into my consciousness. My clients would share how powerful they are. My friends would mention implementing them in their businesses.

One day, my then-wife Meryl and I were driving, and I casually asked her what her business friends were struggling with. She said, "They don't want to hate themselves or their businesses."

Rather than ask her exactly what she meant by that, my brain immediately went to, "What's the positive framing of that statement"? That's when it finally came out of my mouth: Joy.

Meryl's friends wanted more joy in their businesses. And the kicker? That's what I had been trying to write about all along. My business development timeline was a chronology of ways and times I lost joy, AND the ways I brought myself back into it. I had learned to cultivate and curate joy over time.

So, *The 10 Essentials* became *Joy-Full AF*. And I got to writing again using much of the previous book as a starting point.

You'd think it was smooth sailing from there. But it wasn't. I lost joy again. And again. And again. I could not, for the life of me, figure out how the f*ck this was possible.

It took months of trying new structures with my book coach, and exploring even more deeply: *What is joy? What does it mean to be joy-full? And what will make writing Joy-Full AF truly joy-full?*

My conclusions?

For one, I needed to follow *all* the recommendations I was making for you in this book. I needed to have high intentions towards writing a book and low attachment to what it would look like, when it would come out, or even if it would come out. I had to put on the lab coat and experiment with book structures and approaches to writing.

But it required something even deeper than those tools. It required me to ask myself the question: *What does it mean to write a book **my** way?*

INTRODUCTION

I learned over the course of writing this book that my joy gets sucked away every time I try to fit into what I *should* do, and what I am *supposed* to do. I had initially approached book-writing with all kinds of unwritten rules in my head about how to write a book. One was that it needed a linear narrative. Another was that I must use Microsoft Word.

You see, as I went deeper into what joy is, why we're afraid of it, how we lose it, and how we can create more of it, I realized I needed to break the rules of structure and write in "conversations." I also needed to write in a way that didn't require an organized narrative across chapters. And I needed to not open Microsoft Word! In fact, I needed, as much as possible, to not open any word processors or text editors. Most of *Joy-Full AF* was spoken into my phone and recorded in Otter.AI. It turns out, my brain does much better speaking than writing. When I write, all kinds of mental barriers come up that keep me from saying what I want you to hear. My brain also works better when I can feel connected to other people. Speaking allowed me to feel like I was having a cup of tea or coffee with you, sharing my thoughts, rather than writing into the void.

Conversations were the most joy-full way for me to write this book. They were also the most *me* way.

After the winding road the book took, it felt in some ways like I had stumbled into this format. But in retrospect, I was just *finally* coming home to who I am and what I do best: connect with people through conversation.

So back to the original question — why did I write a book on joy-full AF business? The answer is simply, because no matter how much I went down other paths, JOY was always the message that needed to come out of me. Even though joy wasn't in my vocabulary when Niiamah mentioned his World Joy Movement, it has been an essential strategy in my business. It's been what I've unconsciously (and consciously, at times) created and cultivated. And I've seen firsthand what happens for me when I put joy first.

I'm writing this book for you because I understand deeply all the ways we can have our joy sucked away from us. I've fallen into every single trap that you'll read about in these pages. I've also gotten myself out of those traps through the intentional creation and cultivation of my joy. Now, if you're somebody like me, for whom joy wasn't in your vocabulary, or not until you picked up this book, that's okay. I'm going to teach you a new way to look at joy in your business. It is entirely different than what you might think joy is.

I hope that throughout these conversations I can help you see that joy is your business' lifeblood, and the more joy you seek, create, and cultivate, the more success and fulfillment you'll have. Which will also help you create more resilience to stay in your business for the long haul, no matter the ebbs and flows.

So, strap in, let's get some conversations on joy started.

WHAT'S THE MOST JOY-FULL WAY TO READ *JOY-FULL AF*?

One of the most important things you'll learn about joy here is that it's all about you. It's about learning about and leaning into who you are, what's important to you, and what works best for *you*. In joy-fully writing this book, I leaned into my past life as a user experience researcher and leader at Facebook and Microsoft. When doing one-on-one interviews and focus groups with users, researchers often write down insights and themes on sticky notes. They then put them on a wall and move them around until a coherent story emerges about how the product team should move forward in building a feature or experience. I knew at the outset of writing *Joy-Full AF* that I had the equivalent of sticky note insights to share, but that if I pre-ordained a structure or narrative for the book, I'd miss much of what I wanted to say. But instead of hoping and praying a structure would emerge later, I gave myself permission to write a book of proverbial sticky notes that never told a linear story.

Most conversations were recorded as stand-alone pieces. You'll notice they read as such, rather than flowing like typical book chapters would. Still, there is an order to this book; a narrative *did* emerge. Some conversations were about defining joy. Another chunk was about why it's important to put joy first. A handful covered why we are afraid to pursue joy. The two largest bunches were about ways we lose joy and what we can do to create and cultivate more of it.

Within those larger themes, there were conversations that naturally went together. One set was all about ways we lose joy by looking outside of ourselves for answers. Another few covered the relationship between joy and our bodies. My inner scientist got on a roll and wrote several conversations about collecting data and running experiments as a way to create more joy. I've organized those pieces together and added in some introductions to each high-level concept.

If writing *Joy-Full AF* was all about *my way*, I want to invite you to read the book *your way*.

Are you the type of person who reads cover-to-cover, perhaps even in one sitting? Go for it! Do you like to bounce around looking for content that is most relevant or interesting to you? This book is set up for you to dive into any conversation at random. Do you like to read in bite-sized chunks, savoring each concept or insight? Again, these short conversations are well-suited to that. Several even have reflection questions and exercises to help you fully digest.

Whatever way you choose to read the book, may you do so as joy-fully as possible!

What the F*ck is Joy Anyway?

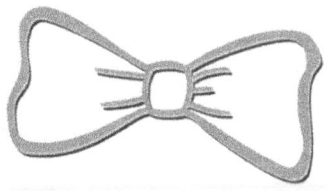

What the F*ck is Joy Anyway?

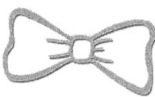

If we're going to spend an entire book having conversations on being joy-full AF in your business, we probably should have a common understanding of what joy is.

If you'd asked me to define it before I wrote the book I probably would have stumbled over my words, shrugged my shoulders, and then — because I often want to have all the answers — rationalized my way into something that sounded smart, but didn't feel true.

It turns out I'm not alone in the struggle to put words to an intangible feeling.

I've spoken with dozens of people across ages, professions, and demographics, and asked them, "What is joy to you?" and "How do you experience joy?" Every time, they pause. Again, it's hard to find language for something so nebulous. As soon as they start to work it out in their heads, they have a similar experience of "that sounds good, but I don't know how true it feels." Though there are common threads in how people define and experience joy, I couldn't find a universal, or even unifying, definition.

Joy appears to be something slightly different for all of us.

As a former academic, I couldn't help but get curious about how academics define joy. Surely the experts could come to more consensus than my family, friends, and colleagues, right?

Turns out, the answer is no. I found multiple definitions, none of which gave me a clear definition of joy. I was struck, however, by a quote from Dr. Robert A. Emmons in the introduction to a special issue in the Journal of Positive Psychology: "Joy may be hard to define, but through the ages, sages have contended that we know it when we experience it, and we know it when we lose it."[1]

We know it when we experience it. We know it when we lose it. **That** feels true to me.

I could have left our definition of joy at that.

But that would have made it more difficult to discuss why we're afraid to pursue joy, how we find ourselves losing it, and what we can do to create more of it.

So, let's at least put some language around joy, using commonalities that seem to ring true for professional researchers as well as laypeople. If you find yourself getting lost in the semantics, come back to your own *internal* sense of joy. After all, that's what this is all about, anyway.

Let's start with an important distinction:

joy ≠ happiness

If you're saying, "Wait, what!?" or you're getting ready to send me an enraged email because Google tells you that the dictionary definition of joy is a "state of happiness" ... hear me out. For every definition of joy that includes happiness, there are just as many that separate them.

The academic research is just as divided. Across disciplines, much of the research has focused on happiness with less attention paid to other positive emotions like joy. Within the study of happiness, there are several schools of thought, and many have differing views on if, and how, joy is distinct.

What indicates to me that they are not one in the same is this: When I ask, "What makes you happy?" and "What makes you joyful?" chances are you'll have two very different lists. That was certainly the case when I asked my friends and family these questions.

So then, how do we draw the line between the two? Again, my definitions of happiness and joy rely on a mashup of science and anecdotal experience:

Happiness is a pleasant emotional state created by positive external circumstances, events, or outcomes, like receiving a gift, getting a promotion, or buying a new car. Once the external catalyst has passed, so does our emotional state. Our happiness levels quickly return to what scientists call our "happiness baseline." (We return to this baseline after negative events, too!)

Joy is an internal sense of delight, gladness, or satisfaction.

Joy is more intense and complex than happiness. And we also feel it on a deeper level — for me and many folks I've spoken with, joy is a full-body, multi-sensory experience. It is often accompanied by a feeling of connection to something outside of us, like other people, the greater good, meaning and purpose, or a higher power.

Like happiness, joy can be temporary. We can experience moments that make us yelp and scream — an active and animated joy — like when we reunite with a friend we haven't seen in years. There are moments that make us feel calm and content too — a more tranquil form of joy — like when we watch the sunset over the ocean. But, because joy arises from within us, it has more staying power than happiness. We can experience it at any moment, and we can create and cultivate it over time. (We'll talk in a later conversation about ways you can keep your joy tank full.)

Now, although happiness and joy are not the same, it *is* possible for situations that create happiness to also contribute to our joy. Maybe we reach a goal we've been striving for, like hitting a $500K revenue target or onboarding 1,000 new users to our app. Maybe we get praise from a client about the impact our service or product is having on their quality of life. Or we attend an event that makes us feel connected to something bigger than ourselves (a purpose, community, or cause).

But these situations that create happiness aren't, and shouldn't be, the only routes to joy. For one, they are unpredictable and inconsistent. They're also spiky, creating a high that leaves us almost as quickly as it arrives, leaving us constantly chasing the next one. Furthermore, happiness is dependent on our circumstances or outcomes *going well*. Talk about pressure to never fail!

I maintain that joy doesn't require our emotional experience or our outcomes to be positive. If you've ever felt a sense of satisfaction or delight while working through a challenge, leaning into fear, or even experiencing failure, you know what I mean.

Joy comes from within you; you don't have to wait for positive circumstances or outcomes to create and cultivate it.

Because joy is an intense and complex emotion, I would be oversimplifying its power if I left the definition as "not happiness." Over the next several conversations, we're going to dive deeper into the foundational ingredients of joy and explore what it means to be joy-full.

THE FOUR FOUNDATIONAL INGREDIENTS OF JOY

Three things stood out to me while I explored the meaning of joy for this book.

- It's a rich and deep emotion that we all find hard to define.
- Joy comes in many flavors. Sometimes it's fun, delight, and play. Other times it's deep satisfaction and connection to something outside of ourselves.
- We all define and experience joy differently, though there are certainly some commonalities.

When I looked at those three things together, I saw a natural analogy with cooking. Like many dishes we eat, joy contains multiple ingredients. For any dish we are cooking up, we have our own recipes and preferred ways of preparing it. It's like we are all at a chili cooking competition, but some chilis are vegetarian and others are meat-loaded. There are red chilis and white chilis, spicy ones and smoky ones. And joy isn't a singular dish we create. We have whole cookbooks full of recipes to choose from.

One of my favorite cookbooks is *Salt, Fat, Acid, Heat* by Samin Nosrat.[2] It's more than a book of recipes. It dives deep into what Nosrat dubs the four foundational "elements of good cooking": salt, fat, acid, and heat (temperature, not spice). You don't need to include all four elements in every dish to produce dishes that taste great. For instance, a garden salad doesn't involve heat. An egg scramble may not have an acid. But at least one element will always be present (usually salt), and typically, the more elements that are present, the yummier the dish.

As I began to piece together the parallels between creating and cultivating joy and cooking, I began to wonder, are there salt, fat, acid, and heat equivalents for joy? Are there foundational ingredients for joy that apply to all recipes for joy, no matter who we are?

When I connected with my own experience of joy, I landed on four C-words:

Connection

Curiosity

Creativity

Courage

I wanted to make sure that these were not just features of *my* experience of joy, but common to other people. So, I thought back to those conversations I'd had with friends, family, and colleagues. Had those words, or synonyms for them come up for others?

Yes! And, I'd been hearing about all of them in different examples, I just didn't realize it at the time.

I also studied how other experts like Rob Bell[3] (International Speaker on Joy), Simone Seol (Joyful Marketing Coach)[4], and Karen Walrond[5] (author of *The Lightmaker's Manifesto: Work for Change Without Losing Your Joy*) described joy. Each of them was talking about at least one of the four ingredients I'd landed on — both Seol and Walrond spoke about courage, for instance — but none of them talked about all four. (I should note that these four C's are tied together as part of 8 "C" words that describe "Self-Energy" in Internal Family Systems (IFS)[6], a therapy model that can be applied in coaching and beyond, but to my knowledge, IFS has never explicitly tied them as a group to joy.)

The more I studied joy and talked to others about their experiences of joy, I became convinced that **Connection, Curiosity, Creativity,** and **Courage** are indeed the four foundational ingredients of joy. That doesn't mean there aren't other ingredients involved at times too. They just aren't as foundational. (Sugar is a nice parallel in our cooking metaphor. It's in a lot of recipes, but it's not one of the four elements.)

We'll explore each in more depth over the next several conversations. I'll also be sharing throughout the rest of this book how these ingredients can bring you back to joy when it's lost, and how they can help you fill up on even more joy over time.

THE FOUR INGREDIENTS: CONNECTION

*"Salt's relationship to flavor is multidimensional:
It has its own particular taste,
and it both balances and enhances
the flavor of other ingredients."*

~ Samin Nosrat, *Salt, Fat, Acid, Heat*

If we are looking at connection, curiosity, creativity, and courage as four foundational ingredients to your recipes for joy, the way salt, fat, acid, and heat are for food, I liken connection to salt. Salt is in almost everything. Yes, you can make food without it, but it often lacks flavor and dimension. Salt has its own flavor, but as Nosrat states, it also has the superpower of bringing out or enhancing the flavors of other items in your recipe. Connection is the same way. Connection has its own unique feeling in your mind, body, and spirit. But when you have a sense of connection, it enhances the other foundational ingredients like curiosity, creativity, and courage (and really any other ingredients that you put into your recipe). In a sense, I don't believe we can have a truly joy-full business without some sense of connection.

When I say connection, I think about it on three different levels:

— Connection to something bigger. Perhaps a higher power, God, or spiritual entity. Or perhaps a purpose or calling.

— Connection to others or to the collective. Perhaps it's connection to the people in your life — clients, colleagues, friends, or family. Or perhaps you feel connected to society, or the idea that "we're all one."

— Connection to yourself. How in tune are you with who you are? What's most important to you? What do you most want and need? What motivates you? What beliefs do you hold? What identities do you carry, or roles do you play in your business and life? How well do you know your strengths and geniuses, or how your brain and body work? For instance, I know my brain cannot create ideas in a vacuum. I need someone to ask me questions or give me something to react to before my brain turns on. And my brain can't seem to write the way I'd like to when I do it in Microsoft Word!

"Authenticity" is a buzzword in personal development work. I've been guilty of using it at times, too. I used to say my mission was to create a more authentic, inclusive, and equitable world. That sounds fantastic! And admirable! But also cliché as hell. What, for instance, does authenticity really mean? Most often I see authenticity defined in terms of how you express yourself out in the world. Are you allowing other people to see who you truly are or are you constantly wearing masks?

I see authenticity as something that doesn't need an audience. True authenticity is when we operate in the world from a deep understanding of and connection to who we are in mind, heart, body, and spirit. From that connection, we can then deeply connect with other people. We can also connect to a higher power, spiritual place, or purpose.

So really, I don't see the three forms of connection as all that separate. And in fact, many people in my circles describe their spiritual connection as something that exists within themselves; that is, their self-connection practice is also a spiritual practice.

What happens when you have a deep connection to yourself? Well, the more you learn about and understand all the ways you tick, the more you can choose *your* way. And that translates into …

When things are hard, you still feel a sense of flow to your actions.

When things are scary, you have a sense of "I've got this."

When it's tempting to go after *shoulds* and *supposed tos*, you lean into your wants and desires instead.

When others want to hand you a map, you trust yourself to create your own.

So how can we create more self-connection? I'm not going to add more clichés to this conversation and tell you to go meditate. (Yes, meditation *is a* way to create connection, but it's also not the only way. Nor is it for everyone.)

One of my favorite ways is to create a map of your internal landscape. Here are a few questions to get you started:

- What's most important to you?
- What are your top five values?
- What do you deeply want or desire?
- What motivates you? Are you more motivated by risk and possibility, or by preventing something going wrong? (Pssst … neither of them is bad!)
- What beliefs, identities, and roles are you aware of?
- What are your strengths and geniuses?
- What do you know about how your brain works?
- What are your natural energy rhythms? Are you a morning person or a night person?
- Do you work better with or without structure?

Once you have a fairly complete picture, ask yourself, "What else do I need to learn about myself?" Connection is an ongoing process. You'll be filling in your map for years to come.

Now, with whatever you do already know about yourself, you can look for where connection is and isn't showing up in your business. What projects, activities, and actions are you taking on from a place of connection? What isn't coming from connection and why not? What are you doing instead? And how is connection related (or not) to your joy?

THE FOUR INGREDIENTS: CONNECTION 13

If you find that much of your business is operating outside of a sense of connection to yourself, it might be overwhelming or scary to think about making a massive overhaul. If you've created your success through actions and activities that are misaligned with who you are, what's important, and/or how you do things, it can be uncomfortable to try another way. Choose one project, activity, or area at a time to make the shift.

THE FOUR INGREDIENTS: CURIOSITY

One of my clients keeps a notecard on his desk that says, "Slow down and get curious." He tells me I said that phrase to him during one of our early coaching sessions together, and he decided to keep it on a notecard as a reminder for himself. It's prominently displayed while he's coaching his own clients.

Another client has a sticky note attached to her computer monitor that says, "Follow curiosity. Have courage." She wrote it after one of our sessions so that upon seeing it she would remember how she wants to show up in meetings, one-on-one conversations with colleagues, and with all the other folks she interacts with in her business.

One day on a call with yet another client (a day she will likely never forget), I asked her to find the silliest hat she owned and wear it as her Curiosity Cap in the lead-up to a sure-to-be-frustrating meeting with the CEO of the start-up she worked for. (I would have loved for her to keep it on, but I imagine that might not have gone over so well with the CEO!) She didn't have any hats on hand, but she did have a full-head-covering mask of Olaf from the movie *Frozen*. So of course, I said, "That's perfect!" It made her giggle — the ideal headspace for the meeting she was dreading. She reflected to me after that it was one of the most open, honest, and productive conversations she'd ever had.

I honestly can't remember the last time I coached someone and the concept of curiosity didn't come up. You might as well call me the curiosity coach!

Sometimes we talk about how my client can get curious about themselves.

That might look like these questions:

- I wonder why I feel so much resistance to networking?

- I wonder why I sometimes have tiny volcanic eruptions in meetings?
- I wonder why a part of me keeps insisting that I need to niche, yet another part contends that niching is business sabotage?

Or other times, we talk about how my client can get curious about their clients or colleagues. That can show up as:

- I wonder what's really going on underneath my client's question about what to do next?
- I wonder what solutions my colleague has already thought of?
- I wonder what might be going on for my boss that she keeps chastising people who are highly opinionated?

And other times, we talk about how my client can get curious about the results their actions could produce:

- I wonder what would happen if I tried this approach to sales?
- I wonder what would happen if I raised my prices?
- I wonder what would happen if I dropped half of the projects I am working on right now?

Curiosity can be an antidote for many of our fears, doubts, and challenges in business because we put ourselves in a place of perpetual exploration and learning. Curiosity quiets the inner voices that are critical or judgy of what you (or others) think, feel, or do. It curbs the need to be perfect, to do it right, or have all the answers. It gives you permission to take risks, experiment, and screw up. And it helps you be less socially self-conscious and connect with people more easily.

Curiosity facilitates compassion, creativity, courage, and connection.

Notice those last three are the other foundational ingredients of joy. I'd say that makes **curiosity** pretty great! In fact, we could use it right now. Think about this ...

Where could your business benefit from slowing down and putting on your **Curiosity** Cap?

And what's one tiny action you could take purely from a place of **curiosity**?

I'm **curious** (see what I did there?! 😉): what could you create in your business if you used **curiosity** as part of your approach in the long run?

WHY IS CURIOSITY SO F*CKING HARD?

If you read the last conversation (*The Four Ingredients: Curiosity*) and you're totally ready to get curious about everything in your world — yourself, your clients, or colleagues, what actions you can take, what results you might create, or what's possible ...

If you've 100% bought in ... you might skip this conversation ... but if any part of you said, "Erin, I hear you. It's all well and good to say that I should be more curious, but curiosity is *hard*," or "Curiosity doesn't come naturally to me," then stick around. This is the only one of the four foundational ingredients that has a follow-up conversation, and that's because it's the one my clients struggle with the most. I imagine that's one of the reasons some of them keep notecards and sticky notes as reminders on their desks.

When I propose becoming more curious to my clients, I often hear comments from them like the ones I mentioned above. They see curiosity as a skill they aren't good at or one that they must develop. I get where they are coming from. I used to believe that too. What we don't realize is that curiosity naturally lives within all of us — we just may not have accessed it in a while.

As I've explored the four ingredients of joy, I've gotten curious about curiosity ... (pun intended.)

Why do we feel that being curious is difficult?

Where does our belief that it doesn't come naturally stem from?

What makes us hesitant to be curious?

I've come to believe that we are born curious, but we get a lot of messages as we mature that encourage us to tamp that curiosity down. If you were born after 1941, chances are you grew up reading *Curious George*. Or you are at least familiar with the monkey who is always getting into interesting situations thanks to his curiosity. Depending on your perspective, George's curiosity serves him well because he learns about the world, or it works against him because it gets him into heaps of trouble that he's lucky to get out of.

Children are naturally **curious**. Babies grab jewelry on people's ears and touch faces to explore tactile sensations. Toddlers pick up bugs and chase butterflies. Young kids ask questions incessantly (to the annoyance of adults around them). **Curiosity** is our innate way of learning about the world, and children display it unabashedly. In fact, we often describe curiosity as "childlike." Little George the chimpanzee is a great example. He breaks rules set forth by adults on the regular. And rarely are the adults, at least in the books I read as a child, joining him in his curious quests. That's because when we become adults, we are supposed to abandon certain childlike qualities and follow the rules. When it comes to **curiosity**, there are subtle ways we get schooled on squashing it.

Let's start with a cliché: **Curiosity** killed the cat.

Damn! **Curiosity** is so bad that it *killed* something. The more that phrase circulates in the collective psyche, the easier it is for us to internalize that **curiosity** will lead you to trouble. It will put you in dangerous situations. It's clearly not a good strategy!

Cliché notwithstanding, let's also look at the language that we associate with **curious** people: nosy, lacking self-awareness, childlike. One of my closest friends, Mahrukh, might be the most **curious** human on the planet. For every single statement you make, she has at least five questions in her head. Because we are not taught how to handle **curiosity** as adults (let alone how to be **curious** ourselves), her questions can feel like a lot. They can feel like an interrogation, though that's never the intention. Her insatiable desire to understand — whether it's a person, a story, a situation, or a fact — can seem childlike.

[Can we pause for a second to notice the negative implications around "childlike" and how it has come to connote naivete, immaturity, or silliness!? If **curiosity** creates joy, but **curiosity** is childlike in a negative sense, then no wonder we're afraid to pursue our joy!!!!]

I believe Mahrukh's curiosity is one of her greatest superpowers. It saddens me to know that others might not agree with me.

Though Mahrukh has been told directly to stow away her curiosity or diminish it in some way, that's not the only way curiosity falls off the radar. For some of us, it's not that we are actively taught *not* to be curious; it's that we aren't actively encouraged to *stay* curious. We aren't given the tools and strategies for *how* to bring our childlike curiosity into adulthood. We don't know what to be curious about, how to assess what is safe to be curious about, or how to navigate situations when our curiosity has led to unwanted outcomes (such as failure or offending someone). The riskier we consider curiosity to be — it killed a cat, right!!?? — the more we train ourselves to choose safety over exploration and learning.

Don't be curious about the people in your life.

(You might ask the wrong question or offend them.)

Don't be curious about where a path might lead.

(You might fall off a cliff. Find the well-worn path that you can be certain leads somewhere.)

Don't be curious about what would happen if you tried that action.

(It's not worth the rejection or judgment you might face.)

As you can gather from these examples, we learn to seek out ways to get the results we want with certainty, risk-free. And yet, going back to the last conversation ... curiosity is the antidote to so many fears, doubts, and challenges.

Imagine the energetic shift of going from what can I do or what can't I do, to *I wonder what I can do.*

Imagine for a moment that you have a goal to grow a following on Instagram, but you have fears about being visible online:

"What if I say the wrong thing?"

"What if I don't add value?"

"What if people don't like what I have to say?"

"What if people don't like *me*?"

So, you spend a lot of time and energy trying to predict what people need and thinking about what to post.

Now imagine the energetic shift if you approached the goal with **curiosity**:

"I wonder what will resonate for people?"

"I wonder if people will like what I have to say?"

"I wonder if I can grow a following by being completely, authentically me?"

That **curiosity**, of course, requires you to lean into risk. And sure, it may kill the metaphorical cat every so often 🙃. But just imagine what you could explore, what blocks you could move through, and what new knowledge and learning might be available if you decided to reacquaint yourself with the **curiosity** you've always had inside you.

Even if you haven't explored it in a while, your **curiosity** hasn't gone anywhere. You can revisit it. You can foster and grow it over time, building it like a muscle. **Curiosity** doesn't have to be difficult. And it doesn't have to be dangerous. All it takes to get started is just one instance of shifting the question you're asking yourself out of fear or doubt into "I wonder" or "I'm **curious**."

Ask yourself, where might you be able to shift the question right now? And what's one area of your business that you could treat like a child in a sandbox?

THE FOUR INGREDIENTS: CREATIVITY

When I think about creativity as fundamental to joy, I picture a five-year-old with red and orange paint all over his hands. It's also splattered on his ears and a drizzle has run all the way down his smock and is dripping onto his shoes. He doesn't care *what* he's painting — he might not even *know* what he's painting — and he's certainly not judging its quality. He's having the time of his life. And his smiles and giggles prove it.

Creativity, like curiosity, is inborn and we most freely express it when we are children. Some kids play "make believe" and other have imaginary friends. Some kids build complex worlds in LEGO®, Lincoln Logs, or Minecraft. (Wait, are Lincoln Logs still a thing or is my age showing? Don't answer that!)

And just as with curiosity, many people have convinced themselves that creativity is difficult and doesn't come naturally to them. Perhaps it's because the word "creative" is often associated with artistic expression. Painting. Drawing. Sculpting. Music. Dance. Poetry. Fiction writing. We judge our own creativity against internal (and sometimes also external) standards of "good" art. If we only look at creativity through the lens of artistic expression — which is often based more on a tangible skillset than creative ability— we are limiting ourselves to studying a few trees in a vast forest. By definition, creativity is simply the ability to *create* something that did not exist before. It could be tangible, like a piece of art, a song, or invention. But it could also be intangible, like a relationship.

The truth is everything in your business is something that never existed before. You are creating ALL. THE. TIME. Perhaps you create a product or service like a course or program. Maybe you create content through blogs, videos, or newsletters. You might create a strategy for finding new clients, growing your community, or broadening your impact. It's possible you are creating relationships with colleagues, clients, and collaborators. Even if you're following a blueprint or a formula someone else has handed you, you are still putting something into the world that has never existed before.

If you've been telling yourself you're not creative, it's time to stop buying into that lie.

We are all creative. We're just not always tapping into the reservoir within.

Just like with curiosity, you can reconnect to the creative spirit you had as a child. You can choose to go back to not caring about the paint splattered everywhere. And you can delight in making shit up and seeing what happens. When you first turn that creativity faucet back on, the waters may not flow the way they used to, not right away. Let it start out as a drip.

Ask yourself: "What's one tiny act of creativity I can engage in today?"

Once you've done that, see if you can get it to drip some more.

What's another tiny act you can do?

Keep aiming for drips and over time, the flow will get easier and stronger.

[Let me bring out my inner psychology geek for a moment on the relationship between creativity and joy. Across multiple studies, scientists have found that creativity enhances our well-being ... which in turn, boosts our creativity. There are various explanations for this ranging from biological (higher blood flow to our brain's rewards center), to psychological (better ability to express and process emotions, a greater sense of purpose). How cool is it that we can create a virtuous cycle of joy and creativity?!]

THE FOUR INGREDIENTS: COURAGE

If you ask my friends to describe me, **courageous** is an adjective that is likely to come out of their mouths. I have done some **courageous** things in the last decade, including having top surgery to align my body to my internal sense of gender, leaping out of corporate with no idea how to run my own business, and writing and singing a parody of Tina Turner's "Goldeneye" Bond song for an audience of 300 on Zoom at a coaching intensive.

People often mistakenly equate **courage** with fearlessness, so they see my **courage** and think I must be fearless. It's really about feeling the fear and proceeding anyway. The truth is, I have been afraid of my own shadow my whole life. I used to let the fear get the better of me. I was anything but **courageous**. Like in 8th grade when I made it all the way to the front of a very long line for the loop-de-loop rollercoaster at Knott's Berry Farm before completely panicking and doing a walk of shame past hundreds of people. But at some point in my adulthood — I don't remember when — I decided I was no longer willing to let fear to get the better of me. I could see how much it was keeping me from joy-full outcomes. I started to deliberately build my **courage** muscle.

When I started to work on this book and explore joy more in-depth, I realized joy wasn't just an outcome of **courageous** action. There's also a joy that **courage** itself creates, no matter the outcome.

Of the four foundational ingredients, **courage** may seem like the odd-man-out. That's why I've left it for last. How can having strength and willingness to confront fear, difficulty, and pain be connected to a positive emotion?

Let's start with going back to one of joy's superpowers: It is one of the only positive emotions that we can experience alongside negative emotions.

For one, joy and sorrow are so linked in our cultural lexicon that you can find quotes on Google about them "going hand-in-hand" and being "next door neighbors." We don't just experience joy alongside other emotions. Paradoxically, we can also experience joy *in* them. There can be joy in sorrow. Joy in frustration. Joy in fear. That last one is what makes courage an ingredient for joy.

What makes courage *foundational* and not simply a nice-to-have ingredient, is how much we need a joy-full satisfaction that can only come from taking courageous action. My friend and former teacher, Sean Smith once said at a coaching training, "The most boring thing you can do in your business is set a goal and then easily achieve it." He went on to explain that if you set a goal and then the whole process of getting there is seamless — no fear, failure, obstacles, or challenges — you won't be satisfied with the accomplishment. Yet, seamless is *exactly* what many people seek out.

We are hardwired as humans to avoid pain at all costs. We often focus on avoiding the pain that comes with fear, risk, and challenge, forgetting that there's *also* pain in dissatisfaction. In fact, I believe the pain of dissatisfaction is more far-reaching and long-lasting than the pain we're often avoiding. To be truly joy-full, and truly satisfied, we need to lean into fear. We need to be challenged. We need to face obstacles and overcome them. We need to experience some amount of pain in the journey in order to bathe in the joy of the outcome. (As Brené Brown has said, "When we numb our pain, we numb our joy.")

We need to feel fear.
It's a signal that we are taking risks.

If we're not pushing the comfort envelope at least some of the time, we aren't growing, nor are we seeing possibilities or creating new experiences for ourselves. There is a joy-full satisfaction that we can only experience when we take **courageous** action and are willing to experience whatever outcomes follow as we go along. To me, that makes **courage** a juicy AF ingredient to explore in creating a more joy-full business!

TASTE THE RAINBOW

There are tons of words people use interchangeably with joy, but they aren't one-for-one synonyms. To me, they are like different Skittles® giving you one flavor of joy, rather than encompassing the entire rainbow. Here are a few, some of which you'll see sprinkled in throughout this book:

Fun
Delight
Pleasure
Play
Bliss
Glee
Elation
Satisfaction
Happiness
Fulfillment
Meaning
Wonder
Indulgence
Gratitude
Warm fuzzies
Hope
Calm
Alive

The good news is, pursuing any one of them will contribute to your overall joy. The more of them you pursue, the fuller your joy tank gets.

What other flavors of joy would you add to the list? Feel free to keep track as we go along.

I SOUGHT JOY; I FOUND ME

During one of the business masterminds I was part of a few years ago, an improv expert came one afternoon to work with about 30 of us. There was a lot of creative energy in the room that day. It was joy-full AF to take a break from serious coaching to play games with my peers, especially because improv is all about showing up without a plan. The sentences that came out of people's mouths ranged from innovative to truly bizarre!

One of the games we played was The Six-Word Memoir. It is as simple as it sounds: Write your memoir (or what you'd like your memoir to be) in six words.

Because I was in the mood for silly fun, the first words that came to me were, *I did it all for my cat*. I'm pretty sure that's because my cat was sitting right next to me, and I tend to rely on my immediate environment for improv inspiration. But then I thought to myself ... yes, we're having fun, but we're also kind of a serious bunch. I was pretty tickled with *I did it all for my cat*, but on the off-chance I was going to be the only person that went down the silly route, I decided to also come up with something serious.

In what felt like a split second, six words flowed: *I sought joy; I found me*. This wasn't some clever phrase my mind came up with. The words landed in my entire body. I had just discovered a deep truth.

Our improv day happened only a few months after I'd realized that I'd been on a mission for joy since starting my business. On the other hand, I'd been (and still am) on a mission to find *me* for much longer. Really, it's been my whole life. As a social psychologist fascinated by all things human, who better to obsess over myself, than myself? I made an instant connection: The pursuit of joy in my business had the unknown (at least, unknown to me at the time) benefit of helping me find *me*.

I sat with that six-word memoir for quite a while after the improv day. I started to wonder if it was actually the other way around. I tried it on for size: *I sought me; I found JOY.*

Yes! That landed in my body too. It turned out that both phrases are true.

When I seek joy, I find more of me. And the more of me I find, the more joy-full I feel.

The moments I feel more joy-full are the times I feel calm, curious, creative, compassionate, connected to myself or something out there in the world, and courageous. (If you're noticing the addition of calm and compassionate, remember that the four ingredients are not the only ingredients of joy and that we all experience joy differently.) It turns out that when I feel one or more of those things, I also feel the most *me*. In those moments, my inner voices like the Critic, Perfectionist, and Controller are quiet. I'm more aware of what's important to me, and what lights me up and makes me come alive. I'm able to partner with my brain, emotions, and body in whatever state they are in. My actions feel aligned and in flow.

I wonder if you have experienced something similar yourself.

What does it feel like when you are joy-full?

What thoughts arise for you?

What sensations do you feel in your body?

What qualities or energies do you feel?

And how does that compare to when you feel most "you?"

Even if your experience of being joy-full and your experience of being "you" differ from mine, I imagine that the truth I discovered for me holds true for you too.

My six-word memoir started out as a personal discovery, but quickly turned into a truth about joy for all of us. The more you seek *you*, the more joy you will feel. The more you pursue your joy, the more *you* you will feel.

Throughout the later conversations, you'll notice a throughline: We lose joy when we abandon ourselves (like when compare ourselves to others, use other people's maps for how to do things, and give in to *shoulds, supposed tos*, and what "good business owners do"), and that path back to joy is always about coming back to yourself.

You'll also notice that this book is about much more than joyfull AF *business*. It's also about the beautiful adventure of coming to deeply know, love, and trust yourself!

JOY-FULL AF, NOT JOYFUL AF (AKA THE JOY-FULL AF BUSINESS MANIFESTO)

Now that we've talked more in-depth about what joy is, let's explore what it means to be joy-full. You might be wondering why I've made up a new word (no it's not just to be cheeky!) when there is a perfectly good term already in use.

Don't get me wrong, I'm all about the concept of being joyful. Being joyful makes me think of sunshine, rainbows, beauty, and big smiles (with maybe a few unicorns thrown in for good measure 😉). Doing what's joyful makes me think of pursuing fun, pleasure, and delight. All good things, right? And all things we do need in our business.

But as I wrote this book and began sharing more about creating joy in business with my colleagues and friends, and on social media, I was shocked by people's reactions.

Advocating for a "joyful AF business" was often misconstrued as selling "good vibes only." It was as if the goal implied by "joyful AF" was a perpetual state of positivity, with no room for struggle, challenge, or negative emotions.

I didn't want people seeing *joyful* as an endorsement of toxic positivity (which is the pressure that people feel to keep a positive mindset no matter how dire the circumstance). I'm all in for joy, but I'm not here for toxic positivity.

So, what does it mean to be **joy-full**?

The Joy-Full Business Manifesto

Joy-full is doing the things that make you come alive, even when they are challenging or make you want to pull your hair out.

Joy-full is feeling connected to yourself, other people, spirit, or even a sense of purpose.

Joy-full is being in the vulnerable messiness of your humanity. It's in befriending every part of yourself and letting them all have a seat at the table, even when you wish you could stuff them down or bury them.

Joy-full is being in your genius and playing to your strengths. It's in seeking more ways to align your business to those strengths, while leaving everything else up to other people who can support you, or simply behind.

Joy-full is being courageous, confident, and fully in your power.

Joy-full is allowing, acknowledging, and pursuing your deepest desires. Even when you know you won't be able to have them all come to life.

Joy-full is knowing that joy is an endless resource within you that you can tap into at any time. It does not depend on external circumstances. (Though, of course, external circumstances can create joy too.)

Being joy-full AF is an entirely different experience than being joyful AF.

I stand for creating, cultivating, and filling up on ALL flavors of joy.

If you've been feeling any squidgy-ness about getting on the joy train, perhaps the concept of joy-full will put your worries at bay.

Why the F*ck Do We Need Joy?

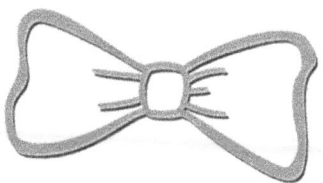

Why the F*ck Do We Need Joy?

If I asked you this question in the context of your overall joy, you might tilt your head to the side, furrow your brow, and wonder, "What kind of question is that? We need joy because we need joy. Period." It's a given that joy is a life force. We are always seeking it in the things we do and the people we surround ourselves with. And we never question others who want to load up on more of it. But this book is about business. And chances are, when you read the question, "Why the f*ck do we need joy in *business*?" you won't have the same reaction. It's not a given that joy is a life force for our business.

If joy hasn't been in your vocabulary around business, it's because it's not in the vocabulary of the business world. Most books, articles, and podcasts about business focus on strategies and tactics. Success comes from things like good product-market fit, savvy marketing and sales, strong leadership, and smart decision-making. If there's any mention of the human aspect of business, the focus is almost exclusively on mindset. Emotions like joy (not to mention the rest of our emotional spectrum) seem to have no place in business.

I hate to break it to you, but we don't leave our humanity behind the minute we step into our businesses. As much as you might prefer to switch off your emotions, it's hard to. It's also not good for your health and well-being. Like me, I'm guessing you started your business to have more joy in your life. Joy in life starts with more joy in your business. If you started it for another reason, think about that reason and see if it doesn't trace back to joy. Financial freedom? Joy. Location freedom? Joy. The little voice inside saying to follow your higher purpose? Also joy!

Joy is not just for right now. As you'll see in the next conversations, if you want to be in business for the long haul, you'll not just need to have joy on your radar — you'll need to put it first.

MISERY ISN'T SUSTAINABLE

Are you successful but secretly miserable? If so, you might be falling into a trap that so many of us do: believing that misery is a necessary evil for creating success.

It's not easy to change course towards joy when we are miserable but successful. Our minds crave certainty, and when we have success, an "effect", our minds search for a "cause" so that we can create that effect again in the future. This means that sometimes we latch onto activities that make us miserable. Our minds credit them with creating our success and target them as essential to replicating that success going forward. We're inclined to believe this is true because it matches the messages we get around "hustle and grind" and "success requires sacrifice" in our culture.

It's easy to see how joy falls prey to faulty reverse logic: If misery leads to success, then joy must lead to … well, everything falling apart. Some of us even tell ourselves there's no other way to run our businesses. We might suspect there is but decide it's too risky to go find out if it's true.

The only problem is, staying miserable is not sustainable.

At best, we might decide that running a business is not for us. At worst, we may find ourselves burned out, experiencing health issues, or even seeing difficulties in our personal relationships.

Which begs the question:

If misery is a recipe for failure in the long term, why not try joy in the short term?

Even if things fall apart, all you've done is speed up the inevitable, and possibly even save yourself some heartache along the way. Once I realized that I'd rather have my business fall apart while being joy-full AF than continue creating success through misery, I was much more willing to test the "success is possible with joy" hypothesis!

Most entrepreneurs start their businesses because they want to get paid to do something they love and have more freedom in their lives. But far too many end up stressed out, overwhelmed, anxious, and ultimately in hate with their business. Like me, they get trapped in the *shoulds* and *supposed tos* rather than staying connected to who they are, what they want to do, and how they want to do it. They find themselves overly attached to external goals and making decisions for the short term that take them away from their joy in the long run. This can look like taking on projects and clients that keep revenue coming in but that don't light them up, rather than putting energy into building relationships that could bring more ideal projects and clients in the door.

The freedom they once dreamed of seems steadily more elusive as they continuously find new ways to shackle themselves to their businesses. You know the expression "golden handcuffs"? Well, I can assure you it's not just something corporations do to keep employees tethered. I have generated a lot of income in my own business by doing things that made me miserable. I've handcuffed myself to my misery, believing my own lie that there is no other path to my income goals. This is why, as we'll discuss in later conversations, part of creating joy is working to shift our focus away from outcomes and back towards the process.

[Just in case you're thinking it: Losing joy is not unique to specific demographics. It happens to beginners and veterans, people working on their first six figures, and those making seven and eight figures, as well as across the spectrum of business types. You can lose joy at any time.]

If you're saying to yourself, "Wait, I'm not miserable, so this doesn't apply!" or "I'm not shackled," you still may be falling into a trap. Instead of misery, you might just feel *meh* — things are going fine and you're far from miserable, but you're a little bored and don't feel very alive in your business. Unfortunately, *meh* is just as unsustainable as misery. There's not enough gas in "meh" to keep the engine running. And it might be a warning sign that you're a step too close to miserable and need to make some shifts before it's too late.

If misery and *meh* aren't sustainable, what is?

I have a sense you might already know my answer to that ...

Your joy can come first.

In fact, it *needs* to come first for you to create sustainable, long-term success and impact.

BUT JOY IS

In case it isn't clear from the book's subtitle — *The Essential Business Strategy We're Afraid to Put First* — I firmly believe that joy must be embedded in your business strategy.

Now, I'm not saying you should *only* follow your joy or that everything will be sunshine and rainbows. Of course, you need a product or service that people want to buy and for them to buy it. You probably also need to be good at marketing, or at least hire folks who are. You also need to be financially savvy and lead good people. But even if you have the soundest of business practices, if joy isn't a top priority, it becomes increasingly more difficult to stay in it for the long haul.

According to the Bureau of Labor Statistics, about 20% of businesses fail within the first two years. Within five years that percentage goes up to 45%. Within 10 years, it's 65% and at 15 years, it's 75%. That means that only 25% of businesses make it through the 15-year mark.[7]

What plays into whether a business is still running past those major landmarks? Google Scholar brings up over half a million hits, with research spanning sound business practices, micro and macroeconomics (certainly the rise of Amazon can be attributed to many smaller brick and mortar businesses shutting their doors!), and psychological characteristics of the business owner (like decision-making, ability to pivot in ever-changing markets, resilience, and courage). As far as I could find, no research has been done looking at joy. And as a social scientist, I don't know how it could be studied cleanly, anyway.

Without actual data to back up my belief, why am I so firm that joy needs to be at the center of business?

Let's fall back on some common sense — can you imagine running a business that you feel miserable in for 15 years!!?? Can you imagine weathering the uncertainties inherent in business like ever-changing macroeconomic climates, recessions, pandemics, or wars without a sense of joy?

I cannot.

Whenever I lose joy, just the thought of not being able to endure in the long term without it is enough motivation for me to focus on getting it back ASAP.

Over the years I've met several folks who have been in business for long periods of time. One of the common threads among their diverse experiences is that despite the challenges of business, their work is immensely joy-full. I suspect if I were to ask them, "What's the secret to staying in business so long?" they might not say joy specifically (after all, it's not just me who hasn't had it in their vocabulary), but they might describe what I consider joy: finding fun and delight, following **curiosity** and **creativity**, and being **courageous** to take risks and try new things. I also imagine they would describe a feeling of being **connected** to something deeper, like a sense of satisfaction or purpose.

To grow and sustain a business, I absolutely believe we should go learn everything possible about making great products and offering high quality services. Our businesses are dependent upon bringing in clients and a commitment to excellent financial practices, as well. We certainly have to be proficient in hiring and forward-thinking in leadership, but I suggest one of the must-haves of business health projection is joy — when you find joy and help your team find joy in all you do, you greatly increase the chances that your business will thrive over the long-term.

IT'S THE WAY OUT OF THE MATRIX

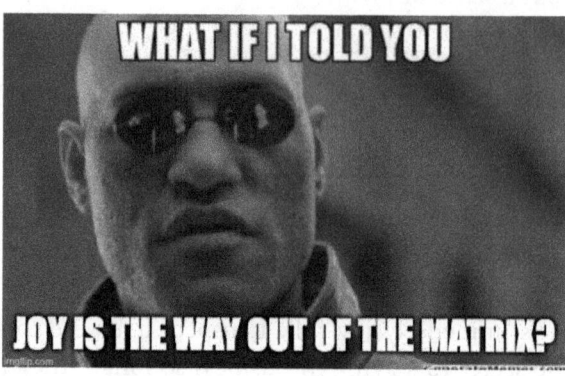

I don't know much about *The Matrix* trilogy, but I do know there is a popular Morpheus meme where people fill in the blank to "What if I told you …" I have that meme in my head as I tell you "Joy is the way out of the matrix."

If you're not sure what I mean by "the matrix", let me illustrate with a story …

"I just don't want to be on Instagram. It's not what makes me come alive."

My colleague, Shaina, spoke these words in a mastermind we both belonged to that was, ironically, all about visibility, and had a heavy focus on social media. We all knew what we'd signed up for, yet her words landed with several of us in the group, including me. She went on to explain that she wasn't looking for us to support her in how to get off Instagram, or how to make Instagram more joy-full for her. She was looking for something deeper: advice on how to stay aligned with her passions and only do activities that light her up. She went on to say, "I'll declare that I'm doing things my way, that I'm stepping out of the matrix, so to speak. Then I'll read an article, or I'll listen to a podcast, or even hire a coach. And before I know it, I'm back in the matrix with a to-do list full of *shoulds* and *supposed tos*. I start to believe that there's a right way to run my business rather than *my* way."

We fall back into the matrix because that's what we were raised in. We're taught that there are right and wrong ways, not that we can find our own way. We're taught who to be, not that we can find who we are ... especially not in the context of business. We're taught to look outside of ourselves for the answers, not that we might have answers within us. Without a foundation of self-knowledge and self-trust, the only place to look is towards colleagues or mentors who we hope will tell us what to do and help us remedy our weaknesses.

Shaina's declaration around Instagram, followed by her share about falling back into the matrix, struck a chord with us because it wasn't news. Each of us in that Zoom room had been deep in personal development for years. Each of us had been (and we still are!) committed to being fully ourselves and doing things our way in our businesses. But, we too had been called back into the matrix. We thought we were the only ones who backslid, while everyone else was doing a bang-up job being and doing themselves. (It's amazing what we hide about ourselves, thinking we are the only ones!)

The neat thing is, all of us have choice. If, like Shaina, Instagram doesn't make you come alive ... or, like my colleague, Laura, you're an introvert and Tik-Tok drains your energy ... or no social media of any kind suits how you like to build relationships ... that's okay. No matter how much advice you hear that you *must* be on social media, you have a choice.

The same is true for anything. Podcast. Newsletter. Book. Ads. Conferences. Networking. Any method can work. It's just a matter of finding what brings you joy, and what feels like "yeah, that's a 'me' thing to do." From time to time, you will fall back into the matrix. Its pull is strong; there is no such thing as a perfect or permanent escape from it. When you do find yourself swept back in, remember that the way out can't be found in an article, podcast, mentor, or coach. The way out is through your joy.

Why Are We Afraid to Put Joy First?

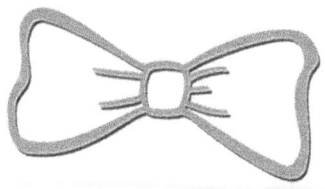

Why Are We Afraid to Put Joy First?

In the first part of this book, we talked about joy being more than a positive feeling. It's about bringing all of YOU — who you are, what you care about, how you like to (and best) do things — to your business. Then we explored why it's so important to not only pursue joy, but actually put it first. So naturally, I must have you convinced, and we can jump right into ways we lose joy and ways we can get it back, right?

Not so fast …

Even if your rational mind knows that joy is the life force of your business, your body may feel otherwise. Imagine a project or activity you are doing in your business right now.

What would make it more joy-full?

Now check in with the sensations in your body as you imagine the joy-full path. Does your body take a deep breath of relief?

Or does it brace?

Do you feel calm wash over you or is your heart racing?

What emotions bubble up to the surface?

Excitement? Eagerness? Anxiety? Fear? Guilt?

If your body feels just as on-board with putting joy first as your mind does, fantastic! You certainly could skip this next section. (Though feelings can change, and you may not always feel so aligned about joy. It's good to have some tools to check in. And perhaps you'll learn some new things about joy along the way.)

If your body feels any sort of resistance or trepidation, that's completely normal. You, like me and many of my clients, probably have some automatic associations and unconscious beliefs that steer you away from joy. The good news is those beliefs aren't innate or permanent. You don't have to keep them.

LISTEN ALL Y'ALL, IT'S A SABOTAGE

It's not just that we're afraid to put joy first. The reality is, many of us don't view joy as something we can pursue or that we can let ourselves *want to pursue*. To borrow the words of the iconic 90s band, the Beastie Boys, "Listen all y'all/[joy] is a sabotage." (Or so we think.)

This brings to mind a conversation I had with Mahrukh, my curious friend from *Why is Curiosity So F*cking Hard?* Mahrukh is a part-time project manager at one of the world's top accounting firms. Don't be mistaken by the label part-time. She isn't working a 20-hour week. She often works more than 40 hours a week, and in her profession, that's still much less than a full-time employee might work. She works this "part-time" schedule because she's a member of the Canadian Women's Cricket Team, which you can imagine requires a sizable commitment. Between the training, practices, and tournaments that demand her dedication, she also hosts a podcast and coaches other folks on how to launch and grow their own podcast. And then much of her remaining free time is spent eating up personal and business development content from people like Tim Ferriss, Gary Vaynerchuk, and Tom Bilyeu, all folks who lean more toward hustle and grind than "find your joy." Mahrukh and I met at a personal development conference put on by business and personal finance expert Ramit Sethi and became close friends after she invited me and two others to create a weekly goals/accountability mastermind group. (Three of the four of us still meet weekly, but we've long abandoned any structure and just connect as friends. Hmm … I wonder if we've followed our joy here? 😉)

By now, you might grasp that Mahrukh is an ambitious, high-achiever and that she is constantly in 'doing' mode. During one of our weekly meetings, she mentioned a quote that really inspires her: "Chase excellence, and success will chase you." Of course, I wasn't surprised. Mahrukh is clearly chasing excellence in everything she does. The conversation led us to a distinction Gay Hendricks makes in his book *The Big Leap*[8] between your Zone of Excellence and your Zone of Genius. Your Zone of Excellence is anything that you are highly skilled or talented at doing, but that doesn't really bring you energy or joy. You may have been rewarded in the past for these things, through promotions, raises, or business success. So it can be hard, even if they don't bring you joy, to leave them behind in favor of activities in your Zone of Genius. Your Zone of Genius is where everything flows and you feel energized. You are doing the things you are *truly* best at and love doing. And it turns out, those are the things where you can add the most value or make the most impact. Your Zone of Genius is where joy lives.

As Mahrukh and I were talking, I wondered if her chase for excellence was keeping her in her Zone of Excellence. Is she disconnected from her genius? And if so, might that mean she's disconnected from her joy?

I curiously asked her, "Mahrukh, what would happen if you replaced the word 'excellence' in your quote with 'joy' to make it "Chase joy and success will chase you"?

She thought about it for a second before saying, "Yeah." But immediately after, her body said something else. She couldn't get behind that version of the quote.

"What's going on?" I asked her.

"My brain immediately imagined me sitting on the couch, watching Netflix and eating McDonald's. It said to me, 'Joy makes you a lazy motherf*cker.'"

I was fascinated by her automatic association …

Joy is the opposite of productivity.

Joy is the opposite of hustle.

Joy is the opposite of success.

Joy makes you a lazy motherf*cker.

We decided to unpack what was going on for her. I asked, "When's the last time you watched Netflix and ate McDonald's?" (I guessed it wasn't recently.) "Is it possible that your brain automatically went to those joy-full things because you've been depriving yourself of them?"

"Quite possibly," she said.

We chatted further to see what other activities besides Netflix and McDonald's she associates with joy. They were all activities she associates with failure and laziness. (And mind you, they were all false associations. There's nothing inherently lazy about watching Netflix or eating McDonald's. We all need rest and pleasure!) Further, none of the activities were related to her podcast, side hustle, cricketing, or work. It didn't even occur to her that joy could exist in any of those arenas.

Mahrukh may be an outlier with her level of ambition, but I don't think she's an outlier in how she thinks about joy. We haven't been taught to pursue and include joy-full activities in our professional lives. In fact, we've been taught the opposite. When I think of the lines I've heard or been fed myself, I imagine a dad with a mustache, thick-rimmed glasses, and an outdated business suit wagging his finger saying:

Quit playing around. You can't be successful with that attitude. Success requires discipline, training, hard work. If you're not careful, you'll end up working at some dead-end minimum-wage job for the rest of your life. Joy doesn't pay the bills. Work isn't supposed to make you happy. That's what your life is for.

The message many of us were raised with is that joy and success can't go together. We've spent years, and even decades of our lives reaffirming that belief. That is, the more we've created success through grit, hustle, misery, or indifference, the easier it is to believe that the only path to success is the one that denies or keeps out joy. It's not a big leap to then tell ourselves that joy has no place in our business and can actively sabotage us.

Without any evidence of a path to success through joy, we're afraid to pursue it, let alone put it first.

> ### TAKE A MINUTE TO REFLECT:
>
> What are your automatic associations with joy?
>
> How does the idea of "chase joy, and success will chase you" land in your body? If it's uncomfortable, what makes it so?
>
> What are the benefits, in your mind, of pursuing joy? What are the consequences? What are some tiny actions you can take in your business to start testing some of your ingrained assumptions around joy and success?

JOY IS UNCOMFORTABLE

Let's revisit the distinction between our Zone of Excellence and our Zone of Genius that we touched on in the last conversation (*Listen All Y'all, It's a Sabotage*). When we're operating in our Zone of Genius, we're doing the things we're uniquely good at *and* that we love to do. Operating in our genius feels easy, flowy, and joy-full. But, as Hendricks points out, we often resist being in our Zone of Genius, defaulting back to our Zone of Excellence. Why is that?

Doing what feels easy, flowy, and joy-full is *wildly* uncomfortable.

We tend to believe that if something is easy for us, it must be easy for others, too. We don't recognize it's easy *because* we have a special skillset, talent, or strength that makes that activity or way of doing that activity come naturally to us. So, in our minds, our "geniuses" are nothing to write home about. We don't even consider them our genius.

We also tend to discount the value of things that are easy. If you've ever said to yourself, "Wait, I (can) really get paid to do *this*?" chances are you were leaning into your genius. Whenever I have asked myself this question, it's always been followed up by negative feelings. This is naughty. Cheating. I must be a bad person. Or, like my friend, Mahrukh, would say, I'm a lazy motherf*cker.

When we're in our Zone of Excellence, activities are more effortful. But that's where we feel most comfortable. We are trained to be hard-a-holics. Taught that if we're not feeling pain, we're clearly not gaining. And that success can't come without sacrifice.

Our discomfort with ease and comfort with effort are not easily retrained. If they were, we would all read *The Big Leap* and walk away committed to staying in our Zone of Genius for the rest of time. Confession: I've read the book a few times and still struggle to convince myself that my genius is truly my genius, and that operating in that zone is the most valuable way for me to impact my clients and run my business. Many of my colleagues feel similarly. Our discomfort (and comfort) is at a nervous system level. It can feel downright crappy in our bodies to be in the ease, flow, and joy of our genius. It can even feel unsafe enough to trigger us into fight, flight, or freeze responses.

I've been focusing here on the ease part of being in your Zone of Genius, but the same principles apply to joy. We discount the value of things that are joy-full. Sometimes, like in Mahrukh's case, we are convinced that they will sabotage our success. We prefer the comfort and familiarity of our Zone of Excellence, even when we realize that the activities we're doing, or the ways we're doing them, don't bring us joy. And like our resistance to ease is at a nervous system level, so is our resistance to joy.

Let's unpack what's happening in our nervous systems. For one, neuroscience tells us that our nervous systems hold onto unprocessed trauma. Those could be "Big T" traumas like a car accident, sexual assault, or physical abuse, or "little t" traumas like bullying, financial insecurity, or damaging messages from parents, which despite being called "little" are no less impactful to your nervous system than Big T traumas. One of my formative little t traumas occurred when my dad yelled at me in my junior year of high school for getting three As and three Bs during a particularly stressful semester, telling me I was going to work at Burger King the rest of my life. It's taken me years to heal from the fallout of that statement.

Our nervous system also holds on to all the stress and trauma related to the societal systems we live in (capitalism, patriarchy, white supremacy, heterosexism, gender binaries, ableism, and more). The messages we ingest get embedded in us below our conscious awareness. For instance, capitalism and patriarchy reinforce traditionally and exclusively "masculine" definitions of success — revenue, followers, user growth (of an app) — and means of creating that success — logic, reason, "smart" decisions, hard work, and discipline. [In contrast, more traditionally "feminine" definitions of success tend to focus on metrics like the level of personal satisfaction, sense of alignment with purpose, and quality of relationships. The means of creating that success are more about heart, intuition, and going with the flow. We need a healthy balance of both ... not just in our businesses but in corporations of all sizes.]

As we've already talked about, we're not taught to pursue our joy. That's because our societal systems thrive on the premise that we'll keep our joy out. What happens if people start pursuing their joy? Will they no longer be as productive? Will our economies fail?

Whether or not you are aware of it, pursuing joy in your business — whether it's through operating in your Zone of Genius or deciding to build a business based on your desires and passions — is an act of resistance or rebellion to these oppressive systems. And anytime you engage in resistance, it naturally can set your nervous system off. Additionally, if you've had any experiences in your life, especially from your childhood, where you were punished for pursuing your joy, you'll have a nervous system response to rebelling even more deeply ingrained.

So it makes sense why you might choose the safe and comfortable route of doing activities in your Zone of Excellence and/or that require a lot of effort and energy, but don't light you up.

But if you're willing to sit with the discomfort of putting joy front and center ...

If you're willing to lean into the ease and flow of your Zone of Genius even when your brain wants you to believe that your skills, talents, and strengths aren't valuable ...

You'll find that joy is the safer and more comfortable path to success.

ZEBRA CAKES, REALITY TV, AND JOY

A few years ago, I served on the leadership team for a multi-day event focused on helping coaches grow their practices. My main role was facilitating small groups to integrate insights from each day's coaching and teachings. I'd been facilitating groups for almost ten years before discovering coaching and hadn't done so in quite a while. Serving the coaching community in that capacity was a no-brainer for filling up my joy tank.

The leadership team met for several weeks leading up to the event. During one of the meetings, we played a game we knew well: What I Don't Want You To Know About Me. Each person shares something vulnerable, that they truly don't want anyone else in the room to know about them. Done properly, it's a great way to create connection and trust quickly in a group.

When it came to my turn, I thought about sharing some "guilty pleasures" like my nearly daily consumption of Zebra Cakes (well, at that point in time) or binging reality TV when my then-wife was out of town. But instead, I decided to own up to something bigger: "What I don't want you to know about me is that I feel guilty that I get to coach people. I can't believe that I get to sit down with people, ask them questions, and deeply listen. I get to notice things about them that nobody else has, and help them grow as people, leaders, and business owners. It feels like play."

That last sentence was oozing with guilt and shame. Coaching felt like play to me (spoiler alert: it still does), and play, at that point in my journey, was a dirty word. Play meant easy, fun, and child-like, which are all things I had deemed "bad", and certainly the opposite of what a serious professional should feel! You're not supposed to play in your job! At least, that's what I had been taught. Work is supposed to be a hustle. It's supposed to be hard. If it feels like play, you're cheating.

Here I was experiencing the deepest joy of my professional life, and I was beating myself up for it.

I was feeling especially guilty because it was spring 2020. We were in the middle of the global COVID shelter-in-place. People were anxious, angry, and grieving the loss of loved ones. Joy was not in the collective. But here I was, full of joy.

After my share, I was amazed to hear I wasn't alone. Not only did others experience coaching as play, but they also wrestled with their guilt and shame around it, especially in the pandemic.

When we pursue our joy, it feels like play.

It feels easy. Like we're in flow. And we make ourselves wrong for that. We've been indoctrinated in a society where play, ease, and flow are too often equated with irresponsible and lazy (psst…this is a hallmark of internalized toxic capitalism).

So, how do we get rid of the guilt? I don't think we need to. In general, I don't believe in stuffing down emotions. And if we do, we border on toxic positivity more than true feelings of joy.

When the part of me that feels guilty starts making noise internally, I mark it as a good sign that I'm heading toward the joy-full path. I know that it's only raising hell because it's trying to protect me from the judgment that might come from other people, from falling into complacency and laziness, and from following what it thinks is a sure path to existential and/or business doom. I let that inner voice know that I hear its concerns and appreciate it trying to keep me safe. (Yes, I talk to the voices in my head. I highly recommend it, in fact!) And then I let it know I'm going to keep pursuing joy anyway.

When the joy-full activities or joy-full path in your business bring up guilt or shame, I invite you to see those feelings as a compass that you're on the right path.

FOR JOY OR MONEY?

Shortly before the pandemic, I flew to Santa Fe for a four-day meetup of 4PC, a small community of coaches and transformational leaders led by Rich Litvin. I had just started my second year of coaching full-time and I was miserable. I hadn't signed a new client in a few months and although the handful of people that I was in the process of exploring coaching relationships with were great, they wanted coaching in areas that no longer lit my fire (namely, leadership and career coaching in tech).

In my first year in business, I had leaned into building my business through the Prosperous Coach[9] method, created by Rich and his mentor-turned-friend, Steve Chandler. Essentially, the method was a way to cultivate a word-of-mouth and referral-based business through genuine relationships, rather than through social media and traditional marketing tactics. To initially get the word out that I'd shifted from tech leadership into coaching, I relied heavily on existing relationships within my network. I was in the very beginning stages of figuring out who I wanted to coach and on what — there were just so many possibilities under the umbrella of "coaching" — so anytime someone in my network was interested in exploring coaching together, I said "Hell yes!" I coached on everything from corporate leadership to career change, to building a business, to personal goals and dreams.

My Prosperous Coach "strategy" was wildly successful for the first eight months. I was well on my way to replacing my multi-six-figure corporate salary, and according to my mentors, my success was coming way faster than most new coaches. But in moving that fast, I also quickly exhausted my existing network. My revenue went to a trickle in month nine and stayed that way for several months. I was still amid the trickle when I arrived in Santa Fe.

I was freaking out about money as I sat in a room full of leaders who were making multi-six figures and *well beyond*. I felt completely inadequate. I was ashamed that I hadn't yet replaced my corporate salary. (In my mind, it didn't matter that I'd made over six figures in my first year, an accomplishment many coaches don't ever reach, let alone in year one!)

I was also disheartened by who was coming to me for coaching. I'd realized that after coaching everyone on everything, I most wanted to coach mission-driven entrepreneurs and small business owners. But the people coming to me willing and ready to invest in coaching wanted me for corporate leadership or career change. The people I dreamed of coaching weren't in my network. At least not yet.

I believed wholeheartedly that I had a choice to make between making money (coaching people on things I didn't want to coach on anymore) or my joy (coaching the people who lit my soul on fire). I truly didn't believe both were possible. And because I was so worried about being enough in comparison to my colleagues, I was tempted to choose money.

What got me out of the catch-22 I'd created in my mind was a single question Rich asked me in a group coaching session:

"What are you willing to sacrifice, let go of, or give up in order to only work with dream clients?"

I didn't have the answer right away, but on the plane ride home it hit me: If it was true that I could have joy *or* I could have money, but not both, I was going to choose joy.

Woah.

When I got home, I looked at my bank account to see if I really could choose joy. *I could!* (Let me pause here to call out that this was a privileged position for me to be in and not everyone has the ability to make this choice.) I made a commitment to myself:

I'm only going to work with clients that bring me joy. Everyone else is a no, no matter how much money they are willing to pay. Yes, I'd like to be replacing my salary. But if I don't make another penny this year, we're not going to go broke. And if I don't make another penny this year,

I have full permission to change course and do something different with my career.

The declaration alone brought me joy. It was uncomfortable to think about making no money and having to face all the good enoughness and comparison fears that were still there. But I knew that I could never run a business long-term if I didn't get lit the f*ck up by it. No amount of money could create longevity if I was miserable.

A few weeks later, shelter-in-place went into effect and COVID times turned everything upside down. Everyone in my circle was panicked about their business. Had I not made that commitment to myself, I might have been too. But I had already come to peace with the idea of not making any money for the rest of the year.

One of the first things I did during shelter-in-place was go Live on Facebook every weekday to give people practical tips for managing the chaos. I also hosted weekly meetups of Facebook community with no agenda but to create connection. It brought me a ton of joy to help people navigate that unprecedented time without expectation.

And wouldn't you know, ideal clients started inquiring about working together. Rather than making no pennies, I ended the year with double the revenue from the year before. Go figure!

It turns out joy and money aren't mutually exclusive, after all.

The Joy Audit

How joy-full is your business right now? Before we dive into the next two sections on how we lose joy and how we can get more of it, take stock of where things are for you right now.

The Joy Audit helps you get clear on what is creating your joy and what is stealing it in different areas of your business. You can answer from a 30,000-foot view of your business, or you can take various elements of your business to do a deeper assessment on (like current clients, marketing activities, projects in progress, your schedule, or programs/products you sell).

In addition to doing the Joy Audit right now, I recommend you do this exercise at least once a quarter, if not once a month. It's quite easy for joy to slip away, so the more regularly you can check in, the better. For a printable worksheet version of this audit, visit www.drerinb.com.

OVERALL JOY-FULLNESS

- On a scale of 1 to 10, where 10 is joy-full AF, how much joy am I experiencing right now?
- What thoughts, beliefs, emotions, or behaviors are making that number so high? *(Hint: Even if the number is quite low, asking yourself what is making it as high as it is will help you pinpoint what is going well.)*
- What thoughts, beliefs, emotions, or behaviors are keeping it from being higher?

- What concrete actions can I take to increase my joy by just 1 point?

Now go through each of the four C's similarly.

Connection

- On a scale of 1 to 10 where 10 is connected AF, how connected do I feel to myself – who I am, what's important, and how I like to do things?
- What thoughts, beliefs, emotions, or behaviors are making that number so high?
- What thoughts, beliefs, emotions, or behaviors are keeping it from being higher?
- What concrete actions can I take to increase my connection by just 1 point?

Curiosity

- On a scale of 1 to 10 where 10 is curious AF, how curious do I feel about what might happen, what I could learn, or what is possible?
- What thoughts, beliefs, emotions, or behaviors are making that number so high?
- What thoughts, beliefs, emotions, or behaviors are keeping it from being higher?
- What concrete actions can I take to increase my curiosity by just 1 point?

Creativity

- On a scale of 1 to 10 where 10 is creative AF, how tapped into my creativity do I feel?
- What thoughts, beliefs, emotions, or behaviors are making that number so high?
- What thoughts, beliefs, emotions, or behaviors are keeping it from being higher?

- What concrete actions can I take to increase my creativity by just 1 point?

Courage

- On a scale of 1 to 10 where 10 is courageous AF, how courageous are my actions right now? *(Hint: we often don't feel courageous. We feel fear. So measure your courage by what you are doing to stretch yourself and take risks rather than how you feel in doing them.)*
- What thoughts, beliefs, emotions, or behaviors are making that number so high?
- What thoughts, beliefs, emotions, or behaviors are keeping it from being higher?
- What concrete actions can I take to increase my courage by just 1 point?

How The F*ck Do We Lose Joy (And How Can We Get it Back?)

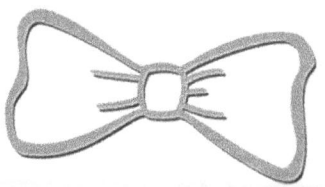

How The F*ck Do We Lose Joy (And How Can We Get it Back?)

Every time I ask myself, "Where's the joy?" in my business, I giggle. That's because I immediately flash back to the Wendy's fast-food commercials from the 80s. If you're not old enough to have experienced them — or if you're old enough but have blocked them from memory — let me set the scene. The original commercial features three elderly women peering down at an oversized open-faced hamburger bun with a *tiny* patty sitting on top. One of the ladies leans in, furrows her eyebrows, and asks in a slightly critical tone, "Where's the beef?" She then repeats it to herself twice more, acting a little more exasperated each time, "Where's the beef?" "Heeey, wheeeeeeree's the beef!?"

I'm embarrassed to admit how often that voice pops into my head. In writing this book I asked myself "Where's the joy?" several times before I landed on a process that worked for me. I strive to be joy-full AF in all areas of my life and business. (Some 9 out of 10 people surveyed and 10 out of 10 pets, not bribed with treats in advance, agree that joy oozes out of me in their presence.) So, few people know that in my first couple of years in business, I lost joy on the regular. By "traditional metrics" — you know, the ones the biz gurus say measure whether or not you're "good at business" — I was successful. My coaching practice was usually full, and at times waitlisted. I crossed the magical six figure revenue threshold that business coaches sell blueprints and formulas for, in my first eight months of business. Apparently, this is warp speed for a business in the coaching world. My income quickly exceeded what I needed to provide for my family. Colleagues told me I inspired them. The sneaky thing about losing joy is that other people don't typically see it happening. And when we're successful by conventional standards, it's often the last thing we want people to know. That makes losing joy also quite lonely. Other than my then- wife, coach, and a couple of verrrrrry close friends, nobody knew when I was joy-full AF, and when I was just pretending to be, in those first two years. And what few people know now is that I still lose joy at times …

Hello, my name is Dr. Erin,

I have a PhD in making myself miserable

while doing the very things

— coaching and mentoring people —

that light me up most.

Lovely to meet you.

Sometimes I lose joy because I fall out of touch with myself: What I care about most, who I want to serve, or how I want to run my business. Other times, I become so attached to achieving external outcomes (like revenue) that tunnel vision cuts me off from my curiosity, creativity, and courage to take risks. And still other times, I get so focused on the short-term goals of creating immediate success and avoiding immediate failure that I lose sight of an important truth that we covered in *Why the F*ck Do We Need Joy?*:

Running a business is about playing the long game. And the only way to be in it for the long game is to put joy first.

Over the next several conversations, we're going to explore all kinds of things that might cause you to ask, "Where's the beef … err joy…?" in your business. Some may feel familiar or obvious to you. Even if you're aware they are potential leaks (or full-on drains) of your joy, it's good to check in with yourself on whether they are showing up in your business right now. Others may be less familiar … or even feel sneaky. You may even find, once you've read through this section, that I've missed naming joy leaks that you know are true for yourself. The ones I've highlighted here are those I know are most common for me and many of my clients. The truth is, if we all experience joy differently, we all can lose it differently as well. Take note as you go along of what you discover about your joy!

STOPPING YOURSELF
BEFORE YOU GET STARTED
(WHAT YOU THINK IS ESSENTIAL
IS NOT-SO-ESSENTIAL)

Before you start any new activity or project, or set a new goal, what do you need to know?

Pause for a moment to note what automatically came to mind.

What comes to mind for me is that I first need to decide whether it's worth taking on at all (I have lots of ideas for projects and activities that never get past the idea phase). Let's start there.

What helps you decide to take on something new?

Do you weigh how much you *want* to take it on?

Are you calculating whether it's a good strategic move?

Or are you already trying to work out in your head what steps you need to take to get where you want to go?

Keep your answers top of mind as I go to this next question.

Once you've decided that something is worth pursuing, what do you need to know to take your first step?

Do you need to know exactly where you are going?

Or the exact steps for getting there?

As you note your answers, notice whether any of them overlap with how you answered the first question.

We can lose the joy of any journey (before we even embark on it) by needing to have it all figured out.

Three of the most common things we believe we need to know are "Why am I doing this?" (My Big Why), "Where am I going?" (My Big Vision), and "How (down to the very last detail) am I getting there?" (My Map).

(Were any of these in your "need-to-knows"?)

When we mentally label these as essential before we even take the first step, we stop ourselves from pursuing joy-full paths. We also create unnecessary stress and anxiety. There are things we just can't know until we get in motion. I don't know about you but wracking my brain for answers that won't come or having 10,000 equally possible options is joy-less. We also lose out on the joy of discovering what's in store for us along the journey. Though uncertainty can be daunting, there's also magic in not knowing exactly where we're going or what's coming next.

Why is it that we see Why, Where, and How as so essential? We'll dive into some specific reasons for each in the next three conversations, but one thing common to all of them is that we don't want to waste time, money, or effort going the wrong direction. That fear is rooted in a toxic capitalistic and white supremacy cultural[10] notion that our worth lies in how much we produce and how much money we make. We can't afford to wander off course when our value and belonging is at stake! So we do everything we can to maximize the likelihood that we'll succeed and in the shortest amount of time possible.

As we go into these next few conversations, keep in mind those other things you told yourself that you need to know before you decide to take on something and before you take the first step. I suspect that some of these steal your joy and that the reasons why they do are similar to what you'll read in the next three sections.

TELL ME WHY
(AIN'T NOTHING BUT A HEARTACHE)

Just because the Backstreet Boys asked you this with their intense eyes and sexy haircuts, doesn't mean you need an answer. You don't need a "why" to pursue anything and insisting on having one can be a joy-ache. (One of my joys is a bad pun!)

When I told people that I was writing a book, the question on everyone's mind was, "*Why?*" Why take on this challenge? Why right now? Did I have a burning message to get out in the world? Was there a strategic business reason to put myself out there in book form?

Early in the process, my book coach suggested I try writing an introduction to the book centered on why I was writing it. I didn't do the exercise. That's because my answer was simple: I was writing a book *because I wanted to see if I could*. For many years, I told myself a story that I wasn't the sort of person who could write a book. Yet, in mid-2020, I felt pulled to do it. Maybe I wanted to prove myself wrong. Or maybe the bigger *why* for my book — and for the difference I want to make in the world through my business — would emerge during the process of writing it.

It felt edgy for me to say that I didn't have a bigger *why* than *I want to* at the outset of the book writing journey. I was worried that people would think I was foolish for spending time and energy on something that many people see as arduous and only "worth it" if there's a compelling reason for doing so. Or that they'd see me as selfish or greedy because I didn't have an altruistic motive for the journey. I'm sure if I had Googled all the reasons why *not* to write a book, not having an answer to the "Why" question would have been one of the top reasons to just say no. And it might have stopped me if I hadn't reminded myself that I've done plenty of things in my life without a big *why*, including writing songs, playing sports, and even a short foray into visual art. I did those things for the joy — because I wanted to.

I could have made up all kinds of other reasons why writing a book was different, including but not limited to, that I was writing it on my business time. But ultimately, needing a big *why* to justify spending time on a project or activity was just a story I'd made up in my head.

If you follow some of the big business gurus you might know of Simon Sinek's famous TED talk, "Start with Why."[11] He's right, to a large degree, about the benefits of having a why before you figure out *what* and *how*. It can inspire, motivate, and guide your action. If you already know your why for any project, activity, or goal, that's fantastic! But if you don't, I want to assure you that it's not required.

We tell ourselves a *why* is required for three reasons:

1. We think we need to justify how we're spending our time and effort to ourselves and others.

    Society assigns value to what we *do* — what we achieve and what output we create. So we feel compelled to only pursue projects, activities, and goals that are logical and benefit others somehow. Doing something purely for the sake of it? Well, that's foolish, selfish, and honestly, downright greedy!

    It's easy to believe that until we can articulate a *why* that passes societal muster, we shouldn't go after it. But here's the problem with trying to pass the societal test for what's worth our time and effort: Who the f*ck is "society"? And who made them Grand Poobah of your choices? How many times have you wanted to try something without a clear reason for doing so, but the thought of being judged by your family, friends, colleagues, or some version of Big Brother in your head stopped you in your tracks? Who exactly is making the rules about what passes muster, here? And why the hell should we be compelled to follow them? Who gets to say that "because I want to" isn't a big enough *why*? *And who's to say that you won't discover a big why along the way?*

2. We admire those who have a *why*.

We see people with compelling *whys* all the time. They could be close friends or colleagues, well-known figures in our industry, or celebrities and personalities. We want to be as inspiring and inspired as they are.

3. We often believe a big *why* is necessary.

A *why* will help us stay committed to our goals when times become difficult and we encounter fear or doubt, or our motivation wanes. Although a big *why* can help us face those challenges and those blocks, it's also only one of many tools you can bring out for doing so. And if finding a big why is preventing you from your joy, that sets up a whole new set of challenges and blocks.

In case it's not abundantly clear yet, let me shout it for all the people in the back: IT'S OKAY TO DO SOMETHING BECAUSE YOU WANT TO OR BECAUSE IT BRINGS YOU JOY!

And, between you and me, it's also okay to do something because the real question on your mind is not why, but rather, why not?

WE DON'T NEED NO DESTINATION!

If you read the title of this conversation and immediately heard the line, "We don't need no education!" from Pink Floyd's "Another Brick in the Wall" in your head, you and I might be long-lost friends. And if you didn't, that's okay. I highly recommend you take a break and listen to the song, because the fervency of their singing matches my own when it comes to the idea that we should always know exactly *what* we are creating or *where* we are going. It's completely unnecessary.

When I say *what/where*, I'm not talking about the singular actions we're taking or the small goals we're pursuing. I'm talking about *what/where* with a capital W: The Big Vision. What does our business and life look like three, five, or ten years from now? We believe that if we don't have a big vision for the future, we won't know what actions to take today. We doubt that we can set useful small goals to pursue or that we can create the success that we so deeply desire without that larger focus.

I have been guilty of believing this, too. Two months into my full-time coaching, Rich Litvin invited me onto his then-brand-new podcast, *One Insight*. Rather than interview his guests, Rich coaches them. He initially coached me on something very tactical — tools I can use to prevent burnout. And just a few minutes into the show, we had already solved the problem I brought to him. We could easily have wrapped up and called it an episode. But he sensed there was more and asked how else he could serve me. I was a bit surprised that he hadn't yet asked me one of his signature questions:

"Imagine we get on a call three years from today, and you say, 'Holy shit, Rich. This has been the best three years of my life.' Erin, what are you up to in your business and life three years from now that would have you say that to me?"

I'll admit, I was also kind of relieved he hadn't yet asked. The truth was, I had zero clue how to answer him. I was only a couple months into my business, and I had no Big Vision in mind. I didn't know what was possible or what I wanted. I was focused on building up a coaching practice, but I wasn't even sure if that would be the centerpiece of my business or a stepping stone to teaching a course, speaking on stages, or writing books. I was deeply embarrassed to be so aimless. And rather than tell myself, "Oh, Erin it's totally okay, you're at the beginning stages, you'll figure out where you're going along the way," I scolded myself for being clearly incompetent and incapable. My inner monologue was basically: "Erin, you need to get your shit together quickly if you have any hope of being successful."

I had seen Rich ask dozens of other people the question. They all had clarity about where they wanted to go. (I didn't account, however, for how long they'd been in business or working towards their vision. In hindsight, that data would have helped me draw a very different conclusion.) So clearly, I thought, it was just me.

Despite my embarrassment, when Rich offered to continue the episode, I asked him to help me pull out my three-year Big Vision. He refused. My inner teenager was screaming, "F*ck you, Rich." But since we were recording for an audience, and I wanted him to like and respect me, I sat there politely and listened to him as he said, "Your challenge right now is to practice living in uncertainty. There will come a moment when either you go, 'Oh my God, Rich, I think it's this. Can we talk?' or, 'Oh shit, Rich, this really scares me. Can we talk?' But something extraordinary is on the way."

On the inside, I was furious. He wasn't giving me what I desperately wanted. And let's be clear about what I wanted. It wasn't just a Big Vision. It was what the Big Vision would do for me. I wanted a sense of security that the actions I was taking in that moment were amounting to something. And I wanted to be able to tell myself, "See Erin! You just needed a little help from Rich to get there, but nothing is wrong with you after all!"

The reason we think we need a what: We don't want to waste time, money, or effort going in the "wrong direction."

(Pssst ... remember, this is also why we think we need a *why*! Our fear of waste sucks our joy in multiple ways.) The longer we head in the wrong direction, the more risk we think it poses to our longer-term success. So, we want to know, "What's the right path? Where am I going?" as soon as we get into motion. We can end up spinning our mental wheels trying to *think* our way into clarity. Often, we waste more time *not* taking action while we wait for our *what/where* to become clear, than if we'd headed off in *any* viable direction, realized "Nope, this is not where I want to go," and then changed course.

Though I gave myself three to five years to build a business that reliably replaced my income from Facebook and Microsoft, when Rich coached me, I was terrified I was wasting time (while also needlessly draining my bank account). I believed that every single entrepreneur in my world (except me) had a solid *what* and *why*. I also believed having both was "the right way" to run a business. The longer I went without either, the more I felt time was running out. Each day was a grain of sand in the hourglass. And each confirmed that I wasn't smart, capable, or creative enough to run a business.

I hadn't yet learned one of the most profound lessons of any goal pursuit: Our map is not the territory. That is, when we start off on the journey, our perception of where we can go or what we can create is based on our current knowledge and experience — which is inherently limited. There is so much more possible beyond what our experience tells us.

If I'd created a three-year vision in that moment, it would've been based on what I'd seen others do or what I'd done in the past. I couldn't have created a complete or detailed map because I couldn't know in advance what was fully possible for me. I also was missing a key lesson about clarity: the more we stay in active motion, the clearer things become. Going off in a wrong direction can be great information about where to go next.

Three years ago, I couldn't have predicted where I would be today, writing this book and coaching my clients. It took me going down several different paths, correcting and adjusting (and re-adjusting), and building a body of self-knowledge as I went along. In hindsight, Rich's refusal to coach me in that moment was the ultimate act of service.

Now I know that there is nothing wrong with lacking a Big Vision. Even as a business evolves, I don't think there is ever a point when one is necessary. And when you let go of needing one, and later one naturally emerges, that can be a joy-full AF ride.

We can find joy in letting go of the need for a concrete picture of what we are creating or moving towards in the future.

We can find joy from leaning into uncertainty and developing a muscle for not knowing more than a few steps ahead.

And we can find joy in bushwhacking our way until we find a clearing.

If you have a Big Vision, or a *what*, I'm not telling you to let it go. One can certainly be useful and nice to have a compass guiding your actions. But if you don't have one, I invite you to sing loudly with me "We don't need no destination!" and to find the joy in that. Have an adventure. Go explore and perhaps find your *what* along the way.

HOW DO I ...

Part of the joy of any journey is figuring out the *how* along the way. So if you're insisting on knowing it in advance, you are missing out on joy in multiple ways.

My friend, Kate, likes to plan every detail when she goes on a road trip. She knows every rest stop, diner, dive, and hotel that she'll stop at along her way well before she gets into the car, and even has backup plans in case of unforeseen interruptions like traffic accidents, inclement weather, or a tired driver. Thanks to technology, Kate can map out a route and exact waypoints to just about anywhere. She really needs to know the *how* of her journeys.

If *"How do I do this?"* crosses your mind almost immediately after setting a goal, you're not alone. Our brains want assurance that our goal is worthy of pursuit. If it's completely new territory for us, or it feels big, overwhelming, or impossible, we think the only way we should say yes to going after it is if we (think we) know *how*. After all, how can we be sure we'll be successful if we're not even sure how to get there? It's not good enough to know only a few of the steps. We want certainty around each of the 100, 1,000, or 10,000 steps we'll need to take to achieve the goal. We want Kate's road trip level of planning, but Kate is mapping based on established highways and points of interest. That makes it so much easier for her to estimate the time and effort it will take to go from point A to point B. She can also fairly accurately anticipate what might delay or derail her plans.

Unfortunately, we want our business journeys to be as easy to plan as Kate's trips. We expect to be on already well-worn paths with easy estimates of time and effort and known obstacles. When we find that the path doesn't exist yet — because we're the first to create a particular product or service, or we're doing something in a new way — we often don't trust ourselves to make our own path. We may decide the goal isn't "worth it" or "smart to pursue".

How many opportunities to go after joy-full goals have you passed by because you couldn't sort out the *how* in advance? I know I've missed out many times! (In fact, even as I write this, I have a big vision for where I want to take my coaching practice in the next few years, but I find the *how monster* nagging me to figure out more of the steps before I commit to fully taking it on.)

Why are we so hell-bent on having the *how* figured out in advance?

I may sound like a broken record here, but again, knowing *how* ensures we won't waste our time, effort, or money going in the wrong direction. We mistakenly believe that if we don't know the entire route (or enough of it) right now, we never will. We can't see the possibility that the path will reveal itself to us as we go along, or the journey itself will create new paths along the way. We also can't see the potential joy that can come from not having it all figured out! The surprises, twists, and turns we encounter when we don't have the entire path figured out can be some of the most adventurous and magical experiences we'll have in our businesses.

Part of the joy of any journey is figuring out the *how* along the way; and really, it's figuring out *your way*. The good and bad news is that the only way to do that is to get in motion and learn what works and what doesn't. Yes, you'll risk wasting some time, money, or effort, but you'll also get clearer and clearer as you go. You'll have doors open to you that you never imagined would, just because you happen to be in the right place or time.

Let's bring Kate back for a moment. By sticking to a pre-made plan, she might not notice the flyer at a gas station advertising a show by her favorite indie musician. All she'd need to do is stay in that town overnight instead of driving through. Or she might miss out on the chance to try a pop-up BBQ joint that becomes nationally recognized because she'd already committed herself to stopping for tacos three miles down the road.

Insisting on knowing the *how* can be a kill joy.

Not knowing the *how* yet can stop you from pursuing things that you're passionate about or really want to go after. It can also create more stress along the way if you don't have all the answers right now and you aren't sure they're ever coming. On the flip side, leaning into, "I don't know how" can be an incredible source of joy. We'll talk even more about the joy-fullness of the unknown in later conversations.

WHO DO I NEED TO BE?

This question is so popular in the coaching industry that it's almost a cliché. It's a question that often follows someone stating a goal or vision that they are moving towards.

"I want to be a best-selling author!" says the client.

"Who do you need to be in order to become a best-selling author?" asks the coach.

I'm going to be blunt. I hate this question with the heat of 10,000 suns. It's a subtle, insidious way to reinforce that who a person is in this moment is not enough, and that to achieve their dreams, they must become someone else. Now this question isn't explicitly asking people to look around at others for answers of who to be or what to do. But ultimately, we are social creatures and that's what we do. Like the client who wants to be a best-selling author and looks to emulate their heroes. We whip or shame ourselves for who we currently are or what we do, while pedestalizing people who already have the personal qualities or professional accomplishments we desire.

It's not just poor coaching questions that nudge us to look outside of ourselves. Gazing outside for validation is baked into the fabric of society. There is no curriculum in our formal education that teaches us how to look inside ourselves for answers or to build self-trust. Even if we are bombarded with messages to "be your authentic self" (like when I worked at Facebook and was told to bring my "whole self to work"), many of us have been rewarded for fitting in more than standing out. We come to believe over time that others have the right answers (after all, didn't it feel like our teachers all had them, even on subjective matters like creative writing?), and they must know something that we don't. For all the "be authentic" messaging, we get even more messaging from family, friends, teachers, the media, and society at large that reinforces the idea that there are right ways to be and do. Most of the messages are so subtle that we don't realize they are running the show.

Our tendency to look outside ourselves is so automatic that sometimes when we do look inward toward what we want, or how we might do things, we draw a blank. Even if we have some inklings, it can be terrifying to follow them. *What if who I am or how I do things is wrong? Then I'll really know I'm not enough.* It's safer, therefore, to stay in the comfort zone of following other people's rules.

"Who do I need to be?" is not just a coaching question I hate. It's also the theme of the next four conversations on ways we look to others that leak our joy. This is one of those places in the book where you might find additional ways you look outside yourself that I haven't mentioned. To be honest, I could have written the whole book on this theme. Joy is about deeply **connecting** to you. There's a multitude of ways to lose that **connection**. The good news is: The more aware you are of your potential joy leaks, the quicker you'll notice them and be able to plug them up!

"JUST FOLLOW MY 10-STEP BLUEPRINT!"

Blueprints.

Formulas.

Step-by-step strategies.

Word-for-word scripts.

No matter what business you're in, someone out there is dying to sell you on *their* path to success. Sometimes, they've followed the path themselves and are convinced that other people can replicate their success. But just as often (or perhaps even more often), the person selling the blueprint or formula hasn't implemented any of it themselves. They are merely a marketer selling something that someone else has told them works. In other words, they are selling you something that someone else sold them.

I regularly get messages through LinkedIn and Instagram from people who are ready to help me get more leads (HUNDREDS per month!), hit my first $10K or $20K month, or scale to six or seven figures. Rarely have these folks been in my shoes as an independent coach. Nor have they created the kinds of results in their own business that they are trying to sell me on some program for. These messages tend to come in waves, which tells me when a new cohort of marketers have graduated from the many programs that teach them how to sell blueprints and formulas to coaches.

Other people's maps are everywhere.

It's so tempting to follow them! The uncertainty we face in business can be excruciatingly uncomfortable. And these solutions promise to take our pain away.

We want to know the right way to:
… design our services or products
… find a profitable niche
… market to our niche
… build a client base
… grow a social media following
… write a book
… make more money

As if there's a *right way*.

This need to "get it right" is ingrained in us from an early age. Our one-size-fits-all education system (especially in the United States) grades us on the extent to which we have the right answers or do things the right way. It teaches us to look outside of ourselves to teachers and experts for facts and information on who we are supposed to be and how we are supposed to behave.

So naturally, when perceived experts offer up blueprints, formulas, or word-for-word scripts, even guarantees, we can convince ourselves that they know better than we do. We feel like we shouldn't trust ourselves or the path we have taken on our own. Why would we take the risk of failing while doing it our way when someone else's right way is right in front of us and they say it'll be wildly successful?

Well … I hate to break it to you …

There is no right way.
There's only your way.

Just because a person has found success with a certain set of steps, it doesn't mean those steps will work for you. Each of us has a unique context: age, gender identity, race, wealth, location, business background, life history, personality, strengths, etc. If no two people are the same, then no two paths can be the same either!

[And even if, by some miracle, you could find someone with your *exact* context, there is still no guarantee their blueprint or formula will work. There's only so much we can control in our world, especially when our business outcomes depend on the behavior and decisions of other humans!]

Of course, our joy is drained any time a blueprint, formula, or script doesn't work. But the more insidious way they suck our joy is in cutting us off from our connection with ourselves and our creativity. When we look outside of ourselves, we don't learn about or tap into our own strengths and geniuses. We don't explore how our brains work or how we like to do things. We don't give ourselves a chance to develop self-trust or to realize that we *can* create success by following our own map.

Now, let me be clear: blueprints, formulas, and scripts aren't all bad. You don't have to isolate yourself from all experts and bushwhack a path entirely on your own. Unless, of course, that's what works best for YOU. That's not what works best for me. I struggle without some sort of reference point or set of ideas to work from. To shift metaphors, if someone hands me a blank canvas, I won't know what to do with it. My creative juices need something to respond to. So, I am better looking at lots of examples of how people have done something and then getting curious about how I want to do it.

If you do want to look at how others have gone about a particular thing, take blueprints, formulas, and scripts with a grain of salt. Especially any that come from marketers who haven't implemented any of what they are selling. The gold is often with people who have been on a journey like yours, but instead of trying to get you to follow their footsteps, they help you figure out what, if any, parts of their path might work for you.

I WILL TEACH YOU TO BE RICH

Every time I try to mimic somebody else in my business, I lose my joy. If you're familiar with the book "I Will Teach You to Be Rich" by Ramit Sethi, that's not who I'm talking about in the title. Though Ramit does sell people "proven scripts", so he's somewhat relevant to the idea of this conversation. The Rich I'm referring to is Rich Litvin, who you met in *For Joy and Money* and *We Don't Need No Destination!*

Rich is known for his powerful language and presence. When coaching people on creating new clients, he offers suggestions on what and how to have conversations. Though he likely doesn't intend for them to be scripts, many people take them as such. Early on in my career, I did exactly this. I figured that I didn't know what to say, so I might as well follow his lead. And of course, if he was giving them to me, *surely* they must work. Even the times when I didn't have a script pre-handed to me by Rich, I'd ask myself "What Would Rich Do?" and something that sounded a lot like him would come out.

The problem was, every time I tried to channel my inner Rich in a conversation, it felt awkward, achy, and difficult. His language — and the power and presence it was meant to convey — wasn't authentic to me. It stands to reason that if being and doing you is joy-full, then trying to mimic someone else feels quite the opposite. And to be honest … it also didn't "work." It's not that Rich's language was wrong. It was just wrong for ME. (And I believe, wrong for anyone not named Rich Litvin.)

We often believe that experts, mentors, and gurus have the answers or know what's best. After all, if they didn't, they wouldn't be experts now would they! Every time I tried to do things "Rich's way", what I was subconsciously telling myself was that whatever way *I* would have done it was wrong. Most of the time I didn't even consider what my way might be. And even if I did, I certainly didn't give myself permission to try. I'd tell myself something like, *"Erin, look Rich has a multi-seven figure business. He clearly knows better than you. That's why you joined his coaching community."*

It wasn't just Rich that I mimicked in my early coaching days. Along with being part of Rich Litvin's community, I was also part of Sean Smith's coaching community, and I worked intensively one-on-one with Christina Berkley. As I absorbed myself in their teachings and mentorship, I found myself also asking "What Would Sean Do?" and "What Would Christina Do?" Rich, Sean, and Christina all had different businesses, but there was enough overlap that I started to create a mental picture about what a successful coach looked, felt, and sounded like. Who should I coach? What should I coach on? What prices should I charge? How should I build an audience of potential clients?

In those early days of working with the three of them, I never once asked myself, "What Would *Erin* Do?" As I soaked up their knowledge and expertise, I never considered what I uniquely brought to the table in experience. Or what I had to teach that they didn't. I automatically assumed that any unique knowledge, skills, or expertise I had was irrelevant.

Hoo'boy was I wrong about that! I mean, I have a PhD in social psychology, for Pete's sake! I don't know *everything* there is to know about how our minds work, but I do know a lot. I know about our emotional system and why it's important for us to feel all our feelings. I know how motivation and goal-setting works, and what barriers we often encounter in accomplishing our goals and dreams. I also know what social psychology research the personal development industry is misinterpreting, and conversely, what research findings are solid enough to apply outside of experimental labs. And yet, here I was looking to Rich, Sean, and Christina to tell me what I needed to know about human behavior to best work with my coaching clients. *cue face palm emoji*

I was also discounting what I learned during my five years in the tech industry. User Experience Research — which was the majority of what I did in tech — has all kinds of parallels to coaching. It's all about asking good questions to gain insights. Often you look underneath what people are saying and doing in a research study to understand what they really want and need. Across multiple people, you find patterns that then help you make decisions about what products to build or how to make existing products better. In coaching, you ask good questions, helping your clients gain insights. Often you look underneath what they are saying and doing to understand the real problem or challenge they are facing (or even to discover the root of that problem). And as you get to know your client, you notice patterns that help them make decisions about how to move forward with their goals and dreams.

On top of being a researcher, I learned a lot about business during my time in tech. I know how to take a product from nonexistent to present on the phones of billions of people (I was part of the team that launched Facebook Stories to the world). That is, I know every step in the process of making a product or service "go live," from initial ideation to exploring and narrowing ideas, to testing a beta version with a handful of people, to launching more broadly. My knowledge and expertise is not something many coaches in my industry — including my mentors — have. Yet somehow it didn't occur to me that it was relevant, let alone a significant differentiator.

I was trying so hard to fit into the box in my mind of "what a successful coach and coaching business looks like," that I repeatedly told myself a lie that I didn't have anything special to bring to the table. The more I told myself that story, the more I was subtly convincing myself that "me" wasn't enough and that figuring out my flavor of coaching and running a business by leaning into my strengths, geniuses, and expertise wasn't going to be nearly as productive as following the advice or examples of others.

And the more I believed that, the more miserable I was. Notice where you might be subtly (or not-so subtly) putting someone else on a pedestal and convincing yourself that success requires you to become more like them. There is no joy in that. (And often no success either!) There's only joy in being you and doing things your way. (And if you're not sure yet who you are, what you care about, and how you do things, there's immense joy in the discovery process, too!)

LOOK AROUND, LOOK AROUND … AT WHAT OTHERS ARE DOING RIGHT NOW

You might notice at this point that one of my joys is titles that reference songs or pop culture. This one might be obscure if you're not steeped in Broadway's *Hamilton*. There's a line early in the play where one of the Schuyler sisters sings, "Look around, look around, at how lucky we are to be alive right now." I can't help but sing that "look around" piece of the tune when I think about this next way we lose our joy.

Now that I've let my inner Broadway star have a moment to shine, let's get into it …

How often do you look around at what other people in your industry are providing their customers? It might surprise you to hear me say that doing so isn't inherently problematic. It can be useful to get creative inspiration by seeing what else is out there. If someone puts a blank canvas in front of me and tells me to paint something, my mind will go as blank as that canvas. I mostly don't generate my ideas naturally from within. My best bet is to gather a bunch of examples as a springboard. Sometimes I'll take pieces of different ideas and combine them in a way that feels good for me. Other times, I'll see what someone else is doing and have a completely new idea spark from that. If that's how your creativity works best, too, go with it!

> Joy comes from working with your brain, not against it.

But know that looking to others can turn into a sneaky leak of your joy tank.

When you look around at other offers, you might find several people offering a particular service. For instance, if you're a copywriter, you might see fellow copywriters selling end-to-end copywriting services for everything under the sun that requires words (social media, websites, email lists, even ghostwriting books). The more people you see offering that service, the more it can feel like, "Well, that's what everyone is offering. I guess I should too."

I've felt a similar pull as a coach. "Coaching" is an abstract concept that encompasses a wide range of activities that someone might do with a client. When I look toward the coaches who are most visible in online spaces (like Instagram and Facebook communities), my brain could easily pick up the message that I should:

- Coach on very tactical problems like social media visibility, marketing and funnels, offer creation, or step-by-step guidance to building a business

- Have one very specific coaching offer or program, rather than a menu

- Coach a lot of people on very short-term contracts (6 months or less)

As a business coach, I do love working with people on some of the more tactical business things. But we do so in the context of pursuing joy, and really in the context of my client being deeply **connected** to who they are, what lights them up, and how they do things. Much of my coaching starts at a deeper level and works its way up into tactical actions. Whenever I start feeling the pull of dropping the deeper coaching work in favor of selling tactical solutions, I know it's time to stop looking outside of myself for ideas and come home to my self-**connection**.

What tips the scale between looking around at others in a way that feels **creative** and joy-full, and looking at others that slowly leaks joy from the tank?

In my experience, it comes down to trust. If we believe that when we create offerings from our joy, people will enroll or buy, it's easy to stay in a joy-full place as we gather external ideas. But if self-doubt, comparison-itis, and/or societal programming about success are running in the background, we have a more difficult time resisting the pull to follow what others are doing. We can convince ourselves that *they* must have the answers or secrets. The more we give into that pull, the more leaks we get in our joy tank.

You might be thinking, "Well okay, Erin. I get the message to not follow what other people are doing at the expense of my joy. But what if nobody wants what I have to offer? What if the reason so many other people have similar offers (like end-to-end copywriting) is because that's what people want?"

I've thought similar things too. But I've also realized an important truth:

If I want or need something, somebody else does, too.

On a planet of nearly 8 billion people, it's next-to-impossible for me to be a unicorn that wants or needs something that no one else does. When I create something from my joy, I naturally create something *I* would want or need. And because I'm not a unicorn, someone else will want or need it too, likely way more folks than I imagine. (Maybe I'm just not reaching those people yet. But that's an entirely different problem.)

If I'm not a unicorn, neither are you.

As I mentioned, this joy leak can be subtle. It's a good idea to make a regular practice of checking in with yourself on how you are using inspiration and ideas from others. Notice when you are telling yourself stories about what you should be doing or what success looks like. See what reassurance your inner voices need for you to come back to **connection, curiosity, creativity, courage.**

COMPARISON IS A THIEF OF JOY ... OR MAYBE NOT

Teddy Roosevelt famously said, "Comparison is the thief of joy." I (much less famously) said, "Comparison is the thief AND source of joy," on my podcast *Life in the And* a few years ago.

In many respects, Teddy was right. When we compare ourselves to people who are further ahead of us or better off in some way (what scientists call Upward Social Comparison), we can easily end up feeling shitty. If we only made that much money, had that size house, drove that fancy a car ... then we would be successful, good enough, or worthy. When we compare ourselves to people who are behind us or less well-off (Downward Social Comparison), we can end up feeling pity for them. Shitty and pity are not joy-full!

One of my colleagues, Jessica, has made jaw-dropping amounts of money in her coaching business. She's been in business just a little longer than me. She speaks openly about her income on social media and often when she does my social comparison pangs arise, and I feel the joy seeping out of my bones. Without fail, several other colleagues message me saying they feel the same thing. Each of us has a very different business than Jessica. Each of us also has different goals and priorities that affect what revenue we bring in each year. Yet, we can't help but fall prey, even if briefly, to joy-thieving thoughts like, "Ugh, I'm clearly not a good enough coach and entrepreneur. And I'm never going to be," Or "Gosh, Erin what's wrong with you that you aren't making as much as her! You suck."

A couple of years ago, I was feeling particularly shitty about myself after reading one of Jessica's posts. She had made $500k that year. My brain immediately went to "you're behind," "not powerful enough," "a failure." Amidst my brain spiral, I read a Facebook post by another colleague, Christine, about how she had been up since 3:30 a.m. stewing about a coach friend. She was asking herself questions like, "How did they propel themselves to success so quickly? How are they more powerful than me? Are they actually, or is that a front?" I knew from the context that she wasn't talking about Jessica. Something whispered to me, "Erin, she's talking about YOU." I immediately dismissed it, telling myself that was quite an arrogant thought. Besides, Jessica's post clearly showed me that I'm neither successful nor powerful. I left a heart reaction on Christine's post and said to myself, "Just be grateful you aren't the only person sucked into the comparison trap."

Within a few minutes, a private message came in from Christine: "FYI you were the friend I was stewing about! Though you know I have nothing but love for you!"

Wait, what!? Here I was telling myself I'm not enough because I hadn't made the money Jessica did and someone else out there was telling herself that same thing because of me. I was letting someone else's success steal my joy rather than recognizing that my success was extraordinary too.

Christine's message, along with my reaction to it, hints at how comparison can also be a *source* of joy. More on that shortly.

So, what's the solution to comparison thieving our joy? Can we just simply stop comparing ourselves to others, as a sea of personal development articles on the internet suggest? Unfortunately, no. Social comparison is just about as automatic as breathing. We humans need to know how we are measuring up. We like to have a way to orient and evaluate ourselves, and to know what direction to go. The problem is, we don't always have the answers we need inside ourselves. So we look to others for information that might be helpful. It doesn't matter what our personal circumstances are — the wealthiest, most successful people in the world make comparisons. We make them so frequently and quickly that we aren't even always aware when we're doing so.

The solution is not to get rid of comparisons, but to learn what to do when they pop up. Once you become aware that you are making a comparison, here are some questions to ask yourself.

Does this matter to me?

Sometimes we make comparisons based on things that don't matter to us. I live in the smallest house on my street by a large margin. I could look around and feel shitty about that. Except I have plenty of space — I don't want a larger house.

Ironically, the same thing was true for my comparison to Jessica's income. That year, my income was much less important to me than having a coaching practice full of clients I loved working with, launching and hosting my podcast *Life in the And*, and managing my mental health through the COVID-19 pandemic and 2020 US election season. If you're wondering why I got down on myself for something that wasn't all that important to me, it's because for a moment I lost **connection** with my internal guidance and allowed societal definitions of success and worth to dictate how I felt about myself. Remember how I said that comparisons are almost as automatic as breathing? Sometimes that's because we have been so inundated with messages from family, friends, teachers, the media, culture, and society about what success and worth look like that they have become embedded in our psyche.

When you catch yourself making a comparison, come back to **connection**. Ask yourself: What do I want? What's important to me?

It takes some intention to unwind our own desires and goals from the ones that have been placed on us by external sources. The more you stay **connected**, the more quickly you realize a comparison isn't relevant, and the less likely it will be to suck your joy.

When you do find a relevant comparison, that is, you answer "yes" to "does this matter to me?" move on to the next question.

Is this reasonable?

If I told you that I suck at basketball because I'm not as good as LeBron James, what would you tell me? That's an unreasonable comparison, Erin! Lebron James is an extreme example, but this is what we're doing without realizing how absurd the comparison is.

We look at people who are masters of their craft, or have been in business for ages longer, or have a previous skillset that gave them a head start, and decide that they are the measuring stick (that we couldn't even come close to measuring up to).

Let's go back to Jessica. When I said she was a couple of years ahead of me in years in business, I was counting full-time. She was a part-time coach for several years before that. She steadily built her business while staying in her corporate career until she got to a point where she could reliably replace her income. I leapt out of corporate to build a business. We started our full-time work in very different places. And, that corporate career of hers? She spent decades in sales and knew exactly how to market herself and her programs when she started out on her own! Her $500K figure was not just a result of more time in business, she also brought expertise to the table. I came to coaching and entrepreneurship from a research background, first in academia and then in tech. I had to start from the basics in terms of learning how to talk about what I do and for whom!

So, what *is* a reasonable comparison? Look at people who are at the same place you are on the business journey. Maybe that's in years in business. Maybe that's in experience they had coming into business. And if there's nobody exactly where you are, ask those who are ahead of you what it was like when they were in your spot.

Be careful, though. Even when you do find a relevant and reasonable comparison, it can still suck your joy. You're not done asking yourself questions just yet!

How am I feeling toward this other person?

Remember I said comparisons can make us feel shitty or pity? Pity is a joy-sucking emotion. When we compare ourselves to someone who is not as far along as we are, we have a choice about how to feel. We may think that pity will make us feel better about ourselves. But what that unconsciously does is tell us that when we are the ones less far along, we are to be pitied. Yikes. A more positive, joy-creating emotion is gratitude. You have to be intentional about where you focus your gratitude, though. Gratitude for "not being where they are" is almost as destructive over the long term as pity. Gratitude for being "exactly where I am" is an opening for joy.

Pity is not the only joy-sucking feeling we can have towards the person we are comparing ourselves to. When someone is ahead of us, we can feel envy. With envy, there is an important distinction to draw: malignant versus benign envy. Malignant envy is a feeling that the other person does not deserve their advantage or status and that you'd like for it to be taken away from them. That doesn't mean you actively wish ill on them, but you certainly might feel some schadenfreude if something were to happen to them. Benign envy is, well, more benign. It occurs when we believe the other deserves or has earned their status and we'd like to get to their level too. Benign envy can inspire and motivate us. It can bring us back into **curiosity** and **creativity** ("How do I get there too?") and help us gain the **courage** to move through fears and blockers on our path.

Just because you have dropped irrelevant and unreasonable comparisons and are choosing gratitude for where you are and benign envy for where you want to be, doesn't mean you are guaranteed joy. There's still one more question to take yourself through ...

What am I making this mean about myself?

This one is tricky. By definition, comparison is about, "Where am I and what does this mean?" Yet, there is a difference between "What does this mean?" and "What does this mean *about me?*" Even though we already deemed Jessica's revenue both an irrelevant and unreasonable comparison, for simplicity let's stick with that example. If I ask myself what it means that she made $500K that year, several things come to mind. It means that she was consistent on social media. That she knew exactly what she offered and to whom. And most of all, that making $500K is possible in an industry where most coaches rarely make more than $40K. If I ask myself what it means *about me* that I didn't make $500K that year, my Inner Critic runs amok listing my deficiencies. I am not successful, competent, powerful, or good enough.

The truth is, what someone else has accomplished never means anything about you.

There are no universal benchmarks of success. Nor are external markers that we traditionally equate with success indicators of your competence, intelligence, or power. I know many phenomenal coaches who make very little money and many not-so-phenomenal coaches who make a great deal. And, despite a society that is obsessed with what we "do", your value is inherent. Nothing you achieve or don't achieve can take that away. You are enough *as is*.

Let's return to the notion I talked about on *Life in the And* that comparison can be both a thief and source of joy. Comparison is a *thief of joy* when you make comparisons that are irrelevant or unreasonable, or when you make a comparison mean something about you. Comparison can be a *source of joy* when you are connected to what you *want* to achieve, rather than what you are supposed to. When you can look to others in a similar place on the journey and be inspired and motivated by them. And most of all, when you can be grateful for being exactly where you are and know that it means absolutely nothing about you to be ahead or behind others.

CONSISTENCY IS *ALSO* THE THIEF OF JOY

Comparison is not the only "C" that is a thief of joy in the entrepreneur world. So is Consistency, though the internet would tell you otherwise. Just a quick Google of "consistency in business" unearths dozens of articles about why it's the key to success. One article goes so far as to say, "even the best business plans will fail without a dedication to consistency."

Here's the funny thing about those articles: There isn't even consistency about what it means to be consistent.

Some examples:

- Be predictable in your brand and/or message. Find an angle or lane and stick with it!
- Show up on a fixed schedule (like every day on Instagram, every Wednesday at 7 a.m. in email boxes). Your client/audience needs to know when they can expect to hear from you.
- Always have a plan for where you're going and how, and have the discipline to follow through on it.
- Have a coherent suite of services and products aligned with your brand.

These all have their merits. But they also have some severe, joy-draining limitations. Let's look at each of them, and how we can take them from thief to source of joy.

Be predictable in your brand and/or message. Find an angle or lane and stick with it!

It's time for one of my favorite phrases: "Yes, AND." Yes, it's helpful for people to be able to easily understand or articulate what your business and message is all about. And perhaps the larger your brand, the more important it becomes to stay narrow and consistent. But for most solopreneurs and small businesses, pigeonholing yourself into a single lane does not allow for your message to grow and evolve as YOU do. Stagnant is the opposite of joy-full!

You'll recall that in 2020, my brand was all about the power of the word *AND*. If I had stuck with that message in the name of consistency, I'd be bored to tears, and you wouldn't have this book in your hand! Because I gave myself permission for ME to be my brand and for my message to evolve, what I'm sharing now is richer and all the more relevant to you.

If you're concerned that you'll lose your audience if you change, I'm happy to report that almost everyone in my community came along for the ride when I did. Some people even commented on how my willingness to evolve and pivot gave them permission to do so as well.

Show up on a fixed schedule. Your clients/audience needs to know when they can expect to hear from you.

I started my weekly email newsletter in early 2021 with the intention to show up in people's inboxes every Wednesday. I've heard from several people that they look forward to my newsletter each week. Now, if I asked them how many times I've skipped a newsletter OR during what time period I sent newsletters bi-weekly instead of weekly, I know their answer would be "I have no friggin' clue." (To be honest, I don't remember either!)

I skip weeks when I can't find something I want to share with my audience. I skip weeks when my body and brain are on the struggle bus. I skip weeks when my schedule is too full to dedicate enough time to writing. If I force it any of those times, my newsletter would be a joy-drain for me — certainly, on those weeks, but perhaps even on the whole.

Rigid consistency / perfect attendance is a thief of joy.

However, what I call self-led consistency can be a source of it. Self-led consistency is when you have the intention for a consistent practice (like showing up every day on social media or once a week in an inbox), but you give yourself full permission to bend and weave with the needs of your brain, body, or schedule. Consistently showing up over the long haul is more important than whether you have "perfect attendance" in the short run.

My commitment to consistency is to show up *mostly* weekly for many years to come. I have to admit, thinking about still connecting with people through a newsletter several years from now brings me a ton of joy!

Always have a plan for where you're going and how, and have the discipline to follow through on it.

The "be consistent" message in this one is all about follow-through. Yes, if you have a long pattern of starting and stopping things, and you know that giving up early is getting in the way of your success, then it makes sense to create a plan and find some support to hold you accountable.

Forcing yourself to have a plan that you follow no matter what is a recipe for not committing to anything at all. This type of consistency is like asking yourself to have a crystal ball. It would be essential to know exactly what goals you are going after, how you intend to achieve them, and have absolute certainty that your plan is the correct one. (Cause, after all, you're going to muster the discipline to see it through!)

I believe the most joy-full "strategy" is having High Intentions and Low Attachment to an outcome (we'll cover this concept in-depth in *Put on Your HILA Hat*). In brief, this means that you hope to reach the goal and will take action towards it, but you also have no attachment to how or when you get there, or whether you get there at all. HILA allows you to stay with a "plan" only as long as it still makes sense to do so, and pivot to different or better things when it doesn't.

Have a coherent suite of services and products aligned with your brand.

Okay, I must admit that coherence can be a pretty good thing. Chances are, if you sell scented candles, coaching, and cryptocurrency, I am going to be suspicious of the quality of any of the three 😉. Even if you're a coach that offers business, leadership, and relationship coaching, I might prefer to find someone who focuses just on business when I'm looking for that support. But then again, if you do a great job illuminating your expertise in all of them, or even how they are all related, I might change my tune. And just because that's *my* preference does not mean it will be the preference of your people.

It's a joy-suck to force yourself to be "more coherent" or hold yourself to impossible standards of what "coherent" looks like, at the expense of sharing more of your gifts and passions with the world.

Where is consistency sucking your joy?

Where is consistency creating it?

And how can you define consistency for yourself in a way that creates even more joy?

THE UNWRITTEN RULES

What unwritten rules are you following in your business? I say *unwritten* because they aren't etched on a stone slab, inked on some scroll nailed to a tree, codified in a book, or plastered on social media. The unwritten rules are in our heads. They're stories we've told ourselves about who we're supposed to be and how we're supposed to do things. That's not to say these rules are fabrications. We glean them from our social world. Sometimes we have been told a specific thing and we turn it into a rule … like "post on social media at 9 a.m."… but other times our brains have filled in a gap or made an inference. For example, if I see a colleague responding to every comment on every post in their Facebook group, I might infer that's a rule of successfully running a community.

We have unwritten rules *everywhere* in our businesses. In fact, we have them in every part of our lives, and we are often blissfully unaware of how often they are driving the bus. (And how much them driving the bus is draining our joy.)

I used to have a lot of unwritten rules about how I was supposed to show up on Instagram (and to be honest, they *still* get me sometimes). When I first moved over from Facebook to Instagram as my main business platform, it was like when I learned how to speak Spanish. A lot was familiar but just different enough that I couldn't quite speak it fluently. So I asked myself, "What are the norms here? How do people do things?"

Generally, it's not a bad thing to pay attention to social norms. We are social creatures, after all! But I suggest we never stop questioning their necessity, and whether we can follow them and still show up in authentic, joy-full ways.

Here are some of the unwritten rules that drove my Instagram bus. (Because we follow these rules as if they are carved in stone or published in a gilt-edged volume, just for the joy of it, I'm going to write them in that language. It also makes me giggle thinking about just how seriously I used to, and sometimes still do, take these rules!)

THE UNWRITTEN RULES

1. Thou shalt beautifully design all posts. Become a Canva pro.

2. Thou shalt always add value. Otherwise, don't take up space.

3. Thou shalt only post "mic drop"-level quotes or statements. If they aren't that great, don't post.

4. Thou shalt have a coherent "brand". Stick to only a few lanes of content so you are predictable and people can easily articulate what you are about.

5. Thou shalt have a visually pleasing and coherent post grid. People don't want to see an ugly display while they are window shopping.

6. Thou shalt do Reels. They must be entertaining AF. That's the only way to grow your community.

7. Thou shalt post EVERY DAY. You're either ALL IN or ALL OUT.

8. Thou art required to share your life, not just your business. People want to know that you are a human. (But don't share too much, lest people think you're a narcissist!)

9. Thou shalt not say things you see other people saying. Nobody likes a copycat. And they WILL know that you are one.

Just look at these rules. To have to think about rules, whether consciously or unconsciously, every time I showed up on Instagram — no wonder I was miserable! Every post or Story, I was worrying, asking myself, "Am I doing it right?", "Am I supposed to/allowed to be doing this?", and "What will people think of me?"

I also remember thinking, "Well, I want to have a social media presence, and Facebook is too limited, so I better get used to being on Instagram. Surely the only way people will be able to receive my message is if I learn how things are supposed to be done here." Let me tell you, when you are trying to "get used to" or "fall in line with" a certain way of being or doing things in a space, there is no joy. And people can *feel* that on the other end. Ironically, the more I tried to make my business appealing through following my unwritten rules, the less appealing it was.

Here's the thing … I made up ALL of those unwritten rules. Yes, there were people conforming to all the rules I had on their own social media accounts, but that didn't mean they were actual rules or that I couldn't be successful doing it another way. In fact, I joined a program from a coach who writes all her posts in her iPhone Notes app. She followed NONE of my rules.

So once you uncover your unwritten rules, what do you do with them?

Well, to start, break one at a time and see what happens. Unsure if there is a hard and fast rule, or just a norm people follow that really isn't necessary? Test it! You can also rewrite your rules. Whether consciously or not, you're always going to be following a set of rules (or principles) in how you do things. And they're going to be made up in your head. So why not create ones that serve your joy?!

Here are my new rules of Instagram:

1. Show up whenever you damned well feel like it.

2. Screw the formatting shoulds. Share however feels good to you. Only prettify a post or do a Reel if you WANT to.

3. Share whatever your heart wants to. The mundane. The silly. The vulnerable. The valuable. If they think you're a narcissist, they're not your people.

4. F*ck perfection. You're a human. The people who want to see your stuff are too.

5. If it isn't joy-full, don't do it.

I posted these new rules on Instagram, in part to hold myself accountable and in part to give other people permission to rewrite theirs. I felt instantly free. Over the next several weeks, I noticed a huge shift towards joy, ease, and flow in the way I felt about social media.

Posting those rules on Instagram also helped this book get in your hands today. Just like I had unwritten rules around Instagram, I had another set of rules for writing a book:

Don't be too smart. People won't be able to relate to you.

Don't be too snarky. People won't take you seriously.

Don't swear too much. People will think less of you.

Be smart. You have a dang PhD!

Be snarky. People love that about you.

Swear as often as you damn well please. You know when it's an appropriate emphasis and tone, and when it's not.

Writing with a set of completely contradicting unwritten rules was not a recipe for joy! When I applied some of my new rules of Instagram to writing this book, everything shifted for me.

EXPLORE SOME OF YOUR UNWRITTEN RULES

My Unwritten Rules of _____

* Choose one area of your business to focus on. Write down any rules you can think of about who you are supposed to be or how you are supposed to do things.

How the Rules Affect Me

* For each rule, write down the feelings, actions you take or don't take, and/or the results you get when following that rule.

My New Rules of _____

* Create any rule that will help you show up joy-fully in this area of your business.

Note: you don't need to replace your unwritten rules one-for-one. Notice that I had nine unwritten rules for Instagram but only five new rules. For me, the fewer rules I follow the better!

SHOULDING ON YOURSELF

Before working with me, Joe had a successful product and user experience consulting business, working with a handful of start-ups. He spoke regularly at conferences and led workshops. He also built up quite a library of videos and blog posts on social media. When we met, he not only wanted to transition from consulting (where he would hand people the answers) to coaching (where he could encourage people to find answers within) he also wanted to get rid of any activities in his business that were no longer lighting him up (and that weren't aligned to the type of coaching he wanted to do).

Pretty early on in our work together, Joe realized that workshops related to design and user research practices needed to be on the chopping block. As were his one-off consulting sessions where people would rent his brain for an afternoon. He also decided (and the pandemic made this easier for him) that speaking at conferences, wasn't high on his priority list.

As he was cutting out activities, we also explored what activities would bring him joy while allowing him to start growing his coaching practice. He immediately landed on virtual coffee chats with interesting people in his network. He loved being able to reconnect with people he hadn't spoken with in a while and getting introduced to fascinating people one and two hops away in his network. Virtual coffee dates were also a great way for him to practice speaking his new business direction into the world.

Within a couple months of cutting out joy-drains and focusing on joy-full virtual coffees, Joe found himself with a full client load of people he was delighted to be coaching. But despite everything going well, he came to me one session with low energy.

Amidst his full client load, continuing to do YouTube videos — a holdover from his consulting days — had become a giant drag. Though it had been easy for him to cut workshops, speaking, and one-off consulting gigs, he hadn't been able to convince himself he could drop YouTube. We hadn't spoken much about that part of his business, so I decided to get curious. What kinds of videos was he making? What were they doing for his consulting business? What were they doing for his coaching business now? He answered that the videos hadn't been much of a lead generator when he was consulting, and they definitely weren't generating any leads for his coaching.

When I asked him, "Then why do them?" it became clear that Joe was trapped in a "should." He believed, based on what he'd been seeing from other coaches in this industry, that regular thought leadership, whether through YouTube videos or LinkedIn blogs, was necessary for him to be successful in coaching.

He went on to share that it wasn't just videos he was thinking about. He'd also been noodling on the idea of finishing his second book. As he spoke about it, I could tell that his noodling was not coming from a joy-full place. I could tell his *shoulds* were also stealing the joy he would have otherwise been feeling about having a full coaching practice.

Since Joe was caught up on what he thought makes coaches successful, I asked him what had made *him* successful, not just in building his coaching practice over the previous few months, but also in creating a successful consulting business years before. The insight hit him instantly. His face lit up and the rest of his body took a deep sigh. Personal relationships and word-of-mouth. The network he'd been joy-fully reconnecting with was created and cultivated by him. Connection is one of his geniuses.

In that moment of insight, I didn't need to ask him what it might look like to follow his joy. He already knew the answer. He shelved the book idea. He let his social media person know that he no longer needed her help — which, to his surprise, allowed her to explore new opportunities with other business owners! And he went back to focusing on meeting fascinating people.

A couple of months after giving himself permission to not create video or written content, Joe came to a session and said, "You know what, Erin? I'm getting excited about creating content again. I like to write, and I'm excited about getting back into it. I may even want to do videos again at some point." When Joe dropped the *shoulds*, it gave those activities enough breathing room for natural *wants* to shine through.

Not every *should* that gets dropped will turn into a want, but some will. For Joe, as long as content creation in any format was a *should*, he couldn't find joy in it. When it was no longer something he held over his own head, he allowed for a natural writing desire to re-emerge.

Sure enough, he started writing content on LinkedIn. One of those pieces of content led him back to a speaking gig. But now he was speaking on something he was really excited about. Will he write a second book? Only if it becomes a want. Will he do videos again? Only if that, too, becomes a want. The more Joe leans into his natural desires, the more aligned opportunities will come his way.

If there is something in your business that you're telling yourself you *should* do, it's probably not true. There are no *shoulds* in business (except perhaps paying your taxes 😉). Anything that you are *shoulding on yourself* will drain your joy. I can guarantee you if it's something that other people are going to see or receive from you, they will feel your lack of joy. When you focus on your wants and desires, and lean into activities that light you up, your joy will be felt by others. Like Joe experienced, opportunities and doors will open.

EXPLORE YOUR SHOULDS

Make a list of everything you *should* be doing in your business. Write each item as "I should ..."

Now go through the list and look for any that you wish felt like a want, not a *should*. Circle those.

Any *should* without a circle, cross off. Those are officially off your list of business to-dos. For anything that is a vital part of your business, like taxes, this is a great opportunity to practice asking for help or outsource completely.

Now, for each circled *should*, asked yourself, "what needs to happen in order for this *should* to become a *want*?" (It could be dropping it for now, changing how you're approaching it, asking others to do it with you. Get **curious** about what might shift it. Get **creative** with your solutions.)

Once you know what needs to shift, make a concrete plan for shifting it. (Example: "I'm going to stop doing X for 3 months and revisit then whether it has become a want.")

ARE YOUR GOALS STEALING YOUR JOY?

Goals are such a big topic within business that we're going to spend the next several conversations focusing on them.

Within the field of social psychology, one of the biggest areas of study is human motivation and goal pursuit. One of the differentiators between coaching and psychology is that coaching is more outcome-oriented. So you'd think that as both a social psychologist and coach I'd be a big fan of goals. The truth is, I have mixed feelings.

I don't think they are always necessary. And when we do set them, there are quite a few traps we can fall into that actively drain our joy, or at best, limit the amount of joy we can experience. At the same time, to feel satisfied we need direction and to see measurable progress. Goals are not the *only* way to meet those needs, but they can be great ones … if we know how to avoid the traps!

"HOW MONSTERS", INNER CRITICS, AND THE KILLJOYS OF LONG-TERM GOALS

Before we dive in, let me be clear on how I define long-term goals. I see them as anything you're looking to achieve at least one year, if not many more years, into the future. Usually, long-term goals are bigger than short-term goals, and require more effort and commitment. Some of my past long-term goals were playing college basketball (Nope, didn't even come close!), getting a PhD (Yep, got that one!), becoming a manager at Facebook (Yep, got that one too!), and becoming a senior leader at a company (Nope! I was on that trajectory but left corporate long before I got there.)

Pursuing a passion, vision, or big dream over a longer period can be joy-full in and of itself. Long-term goals are also a great compass. They guide our actions, decisions, and even short-term goals. They keep us focused in a world full of distractions and quick fixes. And they help us stay resilient during the inevitable twists, turns, and troughs of business and life.

But ... long-term goals can also get in the way of our joy.

There are loads of reasons for this. For one, they can be overwhelming, keeping us from moving forward. The bigger the goal, and the more distant the finish line, the fuzzier and more abstract it feels. Since we are wired to resist uncertainty, your inner defenses are likely to come online to keep you safe. The "How Monster" (the internal voice that wants to know all the exact steps to get there before you commit) is likely to come out screaming. Your Inner Critic is also likely to come knocking, telling you all the reasons why you are incapable of reaching the goal. If the long-term goal is just a little stretch beyond what you believe is possible, the How Monster and Inner Critic are a good sign that you are growing. But if the goal is *too* much of a stretch, you'll likely experience "self-sabotage" along the way. It's not really you sabotaging yourself like you may have previously been led to believe. It's just your inner system going to extremes to keep you safe.

Long-term goals also get in the way of our joy when we believe we need to have them. As we talked about in *We Don't Need No Destination!*, we don't always know what we want to achieve in the distant future, and that's a-okay. I certainly wasn't feeling joy-full back when Rich Litvin refused to help me find my big dream on his podcast. There's no joy in wracking your brain to find a long-term goal if you don't naturally have one in mind. There's also no joy in telling yourself that a long-term goal is necessary for you to be a valid and worthy entrepreneur. And there's definitely no joy in making up a long-term term goal to go after just for the sake of having one!

To tell you the truth, I have just as little idea of where my business is going now as I did back when Rich interviewed me. I've learned in the years since that for the most part, long-term goals are complete killjoys for *me*. So I rarely pursue any.

On the rare occasion I do set a long-term goal these days, I always give myself permission to be committed to it until it no longer makes sense to be so anymore. One of the challenges of long-term goals is that we are making a commitment that "future me" needs to keep from the vantage point of "today me." Who we are, what we care about, and what's happening around us (in our family, business, community, and the world) are always changing. Long-term goals can stop making sense as our current reality evolves.

Sticking to a goal because we've already put time and effort into pursuing it is a recipe for misery. (It's also an example of the "Sunk Cost Fallacy".) It's a recipe for missing out on potential magic. If we're too focused on the goal we're already pursuing, we may not see all the proverbial road signs leading us somewhere more aligned with who we are now.

Still, even if we know there is another, more joy-full path available to us, we can sometimes convince ourselves to keep going, so that we don't come off as flaky or lacking follow-through. (Who exactly are we trying to keep up appearances for? Almost always, it's ourselves. We're afraid of the internal lashing we'll give ourselves for "giving up", especially if we already believe we aren't the sort of person who can follow through on our goals.)

So, should you model after me and mostly give up on long-term goals? Not necessarily. Remember joy-full business is about doing things *your way*. If abandoning long-term goals feels joy-full for you, great! If going after big and longer-term goals feels joy-full, great! And, if you're in-progress with long-term goals, you might benefit from checking-in on whether they are still joy-full to pursue. This next exercise is designed to do just that.

LONG-TERM GOAL CHECK

Long-Term Goal: _____

When did I set this goal?

Who was I back then? What was happening in my life?

Why was it important to me, at the time, to set that goal?

Who am I now? What's happening in my life?

What's important to me?

Is continuing to go after my goal aligned with Today Me?

> [If yes] When will I check in again?
>
> [If no] Do I want to drop the goal altogether or shift it towards something more aligned?
>
>> [If drop] What steps, if any, do I need to take to wrap up working on the goal?
>>
>> [If shift] What needs to shift? And what steps do I need to take to make those shifts?

GOAL TRAP #1 - HEADING TOWARD DESTINATIONS ON OTHER PEOPLE'S MAPS

Even if you've decided, like me, that long-term goals are killjoys, chances are you haven't given up on goals altogether. Short-term goals can give us a sense of direction, at least for the time being, and help us measure progress and growth. That said, there are several joy-sucking traps we can fall into when it comes to what goals we go after.

Unless you are bushwhacking through a vacuum in the space-time continuum, you will inevitably be exposed to other people's maps and destinations. In fact, just by reading these conversations, you are being exposed to my map.

Any time you hear an expert, guru, mentor, teacher, or even a colleague talking about goals, you may be convinced that their goals are "good" ones to pursue. These goals might be truly in service of the people talking about them (or to someone else out there), but they aren't necessarily in service of *you*. Sometimes goals people talk about are completely arbitrary. Other times, they're based on what some abstract entity called "the industry" has decided marks success. (In the coaching "industry" everything was about making six figures in revenue for a while, and now the fashionable goal is scaling to a whopping seven figures.) And even other times, the goals are about products or services they are selling to you directly:

Land your first TEDx talk. It's the best way to build a following of millions.

Facebook and Instagram are dead. If you want to grow your business, it's time to switch to TikTok. (And by the way, here's my course for doing so for $297.)

Make $200K a year as a coach without running a single ad.

These are real examples of social media posts that have come across my feed. They tell me that one of my goals should be to build a big following — though one post tells me to do it through TEDx and the other says TikTok. They also tell me that $200K should be my financial target.

Sometimes destinations on other people's maps will be explicit, like in the examples above. Other times, they will be more subtle. A person may not directly tell you what goals to have, but as you observe their business, you infer that their goals should be on your map.

Inés created a 7-figure business in her first few years. I should scale my business.

David charges $50K a year for coaching. I should raise my fees.

Mark's book sold 60,000 copies. I should set that as a target for my book.

Again, these are real examples. They were all destinations I once thought I should set my sights on.

Whether the destinations are handed to you explicitly or you've picked up on them subtly, you'll know you're in Trap #1 when "should" or "supposed to" starts coming out of your mouth. As we've already discussed in *Shoulding on Yourself*…

Should is a siphon of joy.

GOAL TRAP #2 - GOING AFTER POSSIBLE GOALS

How often have you heard …

"Be realistic."

"Be practical."

"Do what's smart."

"Focus on what's reasonable."

OR

"That's impossible!"

Maybe you haven't heard any of these from other people (though most everyone I know has, often from someone close like a family member, teacher, or mentor,) but I would venture to guess you've said one or more of these *to yourself*.

When we talked about courage as one of the four ingredients of joy, I mentioned that Sean Smith once said to me, "The most boring thing you can do in your business is set a goal and then easily achieve it."

One of our biggest sources of joy comes from reaching and stretching beyond what we thought was possible. Chip and Dan Heath describe it well in their book *The Power of Moments*[12], "We feel most comfortable when things are certain; we feel most alive when they are not." (Aliveness is one of those Skittles® flavors we talked about earlier in *Taste the Rainbow*!) Reasonable, realistic, practical, and smart goals keep things safe, certain, and too comfortable.

At some point, certainty is no longer in service of your joy.

Wait! I hear the record scratch in your head right now. *Didn't Erin just write about how goals that are too big with finish lines too far in the future are joy-suck in Goal Trap #1? That too much uncertainty is bad for us? How can they be talking about leaning into uncertainty now?*

You've caught me. I wanted an excuse to bring back that favorite word of mine: AND. **Courageously** stepping into uncertainty can create immense joy AND it can put our nervous system into massive flare-ups. There's a sweet spot for every one of us, where uncertainty goes from feeling uncomfortable to feeling unsafe for our systems. (We'll talk about this sweet spot more in *Uncomfortable Versus Unsafe*.)

When I advocate for setting goals that are unreasonable, impractical, or even feel impossible, I'm not advocating for setting big, hairy audacious long-term goals. Smaller, more short-term goals can also feel impossible! (I could feel it's impossible to sell out my next group coaching program, or to get booked as a guest on one of my favorite podcasts.)

I'm *also* not advocating for setting goals that are way beyond what you or your nervous system is capable of right now. For me, one guidepost is a stretch that feels just on the other side of possible. Adrienne Mishler of the popular YouTube series *Yoga with Adrienne* calls it "finding your appropriate edge." Landing a publishing deal for my second book might feel impossible, but not so ridiculous as to flare my system. But becoming as well-known as Brené Brown or Glennon Doyle might be a whole different story!

Now, I'm not saying that you should avoid realistic or possible goals. Wins can boost your confidence. (And sometimes you need the resources, whether monetary or emotional to be able to move forward joy-fully.) But if you find yourself bored or joyless with your goals, chances are you're playing too much in the realm of possible and could use a stretch.

GOAL TRAP #3 - CHASING HAPPINESS

Raise your hand if you've ever said ... "When I reach goal X, I will be happy"? I know I have!

When we defined joy, I explicitly called out the difference between joy and happiness. If you've wondered why it was important to make that distinction, it's because of this goal trap.

Recall that we've defined happiness as a pleasant emotional state caused by a positive outcome or circumstance. So achieving a goal could be a source of happiness. We're not lying to ourselves when we think, "When I accomplish this goal, I will be happy." The problem is, happiness is fleeting. Once it dissipates and we move back to a general baseline of happiness, we chase the high again by dangling another carrot in front ourselves. In other words, setting a new goal. Psychologists call this the Hedonic Treadmill. No one wants just a temporary high. Yet, when we chase happiness, we don't necessarily see that's what we are settling for.

It's easy to get tunnel vision when we chase happiness. We are so focused on the feeling that is to come in the future, that we forget to tune into the feelings we are having right now. (Which means we're not tuning into joy, nor are we deliberately creating it!) We can even tell ourselves that any misery we're experiencing on the way to a goal is a worthy sacrifice, in order to have the happiness payoff later.

Be careful not to chase happiness at the expense of your joy.

Joy doesn't rely on you reaching a destination or accomplishing a goal. Or on any other circumstance, for that matter. It's a resource within you that you can tap into at *any time*. And you can cultivate more of it over time. As you continuously fill your joy tank, it expands to hold even more. You can be joy-full in success, joy-full in failure, and joy-full at any step along the way.

So rather than chase goals that will make you happy at some later date, instead set goals that feel joy-full now, and will continue to be every step of the way.

GOAL TRAP #4 - CHASING ENOUGHNESS

In my opinion, chasing the feeling of enoughness is the most insidious of all the joy traps because it hits us in our most tender and vulnerable spots. That's why I've saved it for last.

When we say, "When I reach X goal, then I will be ... ", happy is not the only word we use to finish that sentence. We have all kinds of things we hope achieving a goal will do for us:

When I make $150,000 a year in my business, I will be able to call myself a successful massage therapist.

When I get selected for a TED talk, I will know my story is valuable and therefore I am valuable.

When I receive venture capital funding for my start-up I will know I am a capable innovator.

I believe avoiding this trap is impossible. We need positive self-worth for our mental and emotional well-being the way our bodies need food, water, and sleep. No matter our current sense of self-worth, our brains always reach for ways to either increase or preserve our enoughness. Achieving goals is one of the ways our brains try to do this. Even if we're able to recognize this as a faulty strategy, in a society that judges and values people for what they do, it can be difficult to permanently override our automatic association between value, worth, and achievement.

We may not be able to completely avoid this trap, but we can recognize when we've fallen into it and learn how to pull ourselves back out.

Trap #4, then, is about what our brains are convinced our goal will do for our self-worth. "When I achieve this goal, I will be _____." Fill in the blank: successful? capable? competent? good enough?

Really, these all boil down to chasing our enoughness. If I am successful, I am enough. If am capable, I am enough. If I am competent, I am enough. You get the idea.

The problem with this strategy is that if we believe *achieving* the goal will grant us enoughness, the flipside must also be true: *failing* to reach the goal signals that we are not successful, capable, competent, worthy … or enough. Talk about pressure to never fail!

Though we might think that avoiding failure is avoiding judgment from others, we're really (understandably) avoiding feeling embarrassed and ashamed of ourselves. We don't want to face the lashings of our Inner Critic, who can be quite good at convincing us that we're a shitty human being!

You'll never be enough.

Who did you think you were to try to do that?

You're pitiful.

You might as well give up now. Loser.

Everyone thinks that you're incompetent. You might as well accept that.

When we have our whole self-worth riding on accomplishing specific goals, we clench to them. We become needy. We get tunnel vision. We become risk averse. We get hell-bent on reaching that destination, even if it makes us miserable in the process.

There is no room for joy when you are chasing your enoughness.

TAKE A MINUTE TO REFLECT:

What goals would you set if you knew that reaching them meant nothing about your success, capability, or competence?

What goals would you set if you knew that you were enough no matter what?

FALLING INTO MULTIPLE TRAPS AT ONCE

The traps we've covered in the last few conversations are not mutually exclusive. In fact, in my experience, it's common to fall into multiple at once (or even all four of them). We can set a goal that feels reasonably attainable (Trap #2), based on what someone else has gone after, or has indicated is a measure of success (Trap #1), and clench to that goal because we've decided that reaching it will mean that we're successful (Trap #4) and that we'll be happy (Trap #3).

What an epic joy-suck to take someone else's definition of success — which is personal to them at best, and completely arbitrary at worst — and tell ourselves that we aren't successful unless we meet it.

Let's use revenue to illustrate. It's one of the most universal goals of entrepreneurs AND one I constantly see siphoning joy (my own included). As I mentioned in *Just Follow My 10-Step Blueprint!*, coaches are flooded with messages about creating their first six figures, or even scaling to seven figures.

When I first started coaching, there was a revenue number that seemed to be commonly tossed around in multiple peer circles. I quickly anchored into it as a marker of success (Trap #1). It was also basically what I was making at Microsoft, so replacing my income felt reasonable (Trap #2), like a real marker of whether I was a competent, capable, good enough coach and entrepreneur (Trap #4), and a recipe for happiness (Trap #3).

I didn't once ask myself ...

"What level of revenue do I *want?*"

"Do I need that amount of money to live the life I now want? The one I left corporate to create?"

"Is that amount aligned with the kinds of activities I want to be doing in my business?"

"Is it aligned with the effort and time I want to be putting into my business?"

I also didn't consider if revenue was a primary goal of mine, or if there were other, dare I say, more joy-full goals I could focus on that would lead to a comfortable income.

I became so needy, clenching around replacing my corporate salary that I made all kinds of misery-inducing choices. I took on clients who were less joy-full to work with. Don't get me wrong, I love most human beings, but sometimes people aren't ready for the depth of work I do. And certain areas of focus in coaching are more exciting for me than others. I said yes to people and focus areas that I knew weren't a fit. I also took on too many clients, prioritizing money in the bank over what my energetic capacity could handle. To make matters worse, I often designed creative coaching agreements to make it more affordable for people to work with me (like meeting monthly rather than biweekly), which meant I was tapping myself out energetically AND *still struggling to meet my revenue targets.*

I also designed several coaching programs that I thought would be easy yeses for folks but that didn't totally light up my heart and soul to deliver. One of those programs was The Launch Accelerator for new business owners. The program itself was well-designed (or so said my peers at the time) and was a "*good business decision.*" But it wasn't a joy-full decision for me. And my energy around marketing it and enrolling people showed it. I didn't get a single taker.

I've since become aware of all four traps I can fall into with goal setting and have been more intentional with checking in on what feels joy-full to pursue, rather than what will make me "successful", "good enough", and (momentarily) happy.

Now that you know about these traps, the next exercise will help you get clear on which, if any, you are falling into, and how you can pull yourself back out of them. I get that this could be overwhelming. You DO NOT need to do all your goals at once.

FALLING INTO MULTIPLE TRAPS AT ONCE

Choose which one (or two) feels good or important to work with right now. You can always come back to others later.

GOAL TRAPS CHECK-IN

My Goal_____:

Did I come up with this goal or learn it elsewhere? If I learned it from someone else, is it a goal I want to keep?

How realistic or possible is this goal?

    If it feels possible, then: Is this a goal I want to stretch on?

        [If yes] What would feel like a good stretch? (Check in with your body to make sure the stretch doesn't feel overwhelming to your nervous system.)

        [If no] There's nothing else to do. Keep on keeping on.

    If it already feels impossible, check in with your body: Does this stretch feel uncomfortable but something I can lean into, or does it feel overwhelming to my nervous system?

What am I making achieving this goal mean about me? What does it actually mean?

To what extent is my happiness riding on achieving this goal? How can I let go of that need and focus more on my joy?

If it's too much, how can I dial back the goal to something that feels safer in my nervous system?

MORE MORE MORE

"I could be doing more!" If there's one phrase that's on repeat in the heads of most business owners I know, it's this one.

There is always so much more we could be doing in our business. In a world with thousands of options and pathways to success, that statement is *technically* true. The problem is, we often translate that into "There's so much more I *should* be doing."

Over the last several years, most of my coaching clients have come to me through word-of-mouth and referral. I could continue to rely on my current clients to refer new ones, but I don't want my clients to be solely responsible for my business success. Don't get me wrong — I love referrals! But I also prefer for them to be a delight, rather than something I'm wishing and hoping will happen to keep my business full.

So if I want to bring more clients into my coaching world, I have several options:

- Go to in-person events in Ann Arbor and Ypsilanti.
- Go a little further down the road to in-person events in Detroit and its surrounding metro area.
- Attend conferences and trainings, virtually and in-person.
- Host a podcast. (Which I did for a while with *Life in the And* and *Shift-Starters*.)
- Build a following on social media. (Which I've started to focus on more recently.)
- Cultivate a community through email. (Which I do! I write a weekly newsletter.)
- Write articles for *Forbes*, *Entrepreneur*, or other large media publishers.
- Do a TED talk.
- Get on the speaking circuit.

And those are just a *few* of the options. When I tell myself that I need to be doing more than a couple of these strategies — or when I tell myself I'm not doing any one strategy enough — I quickly lose joy.

My need to do more is rooted in fear. There's so much information out there about what strategies are THE ticket to success. I've seen business gurus say, "If you're not doing a podcast, what are you doing with your business?" I've seen others say the same about social media. On the flip side, I've heard people say, "You know what? Social media is a volatile thing. The algorithm is always changing and not always in your favor. And what happens if social disappears one day? You're better off having an email newsletter."

When I'm not taking a step back and asking, "What path feels most joy-full?" I can get lost in a sea of options, and I can easily end up with the thought, "I should do all of them. That way I can cover my bases in case any one of them doesn't work."

Then when I try to do too much, I burn out. I don't want to do any of it. And when I do the work anyway, my energy is not loving, caring, or joy-full.

Where are you convincing yourself that more is better? Where are you risking overwhelm, burnout, or failure by doing too many things? What would happen if you chose to focus on just a few things at a time instead?

HELLO, IT'S ME, YOUR NERVOUS SYSTEM

Let's revisit part of our definition of joy for a moment (see *What the F*ck is Joy Anyway?* for a refresher): It's a *full-body* experience. Our bodies, and more specifically our nervous systems, have a large role to play in our joy — in how we feel it, create it, and cultivate it. And when we ignore or override our bodies, we crowd out joy.

Throughout most of human history, the mind-body connection was a given. It wasn't well understood, but it was a premise of all medicine and healing. However, during the 17th century, the "Western world" began to see the mind and body as separate entities and started referring to the body as if it were more machine-like. Thanks to colonialism, that notion of mind-body separation spread and became the dominant paradigm for a large part of the world. As part of this, society came to reward thought over emotion, logic and reason over intuition, and intellect over instinct.

That said, the tides are beginning to turn. Eastern medicine, spirituality, and mindfulness practices are becoming more mainstream. Western medicine is beginning to adopt healing modalities like acupuncture that were once written off as junk. Neuroscientists are discovering more and more about how our nervous system affects everything from bodily functions (like digestion) and drives (like hunger) to our thoughts, feelings, and behaviors.

Although science's understanding of the mind-body connection continues to improve, society has not yet shifted from over-rewarding thought, logic, reason, and intellect. Most of us have been raised to distrust our bodies and ignore its signals. We believe our bodies are supposed to function like machines, letting us produce consistently across time (day-to-day, week-to-week, month-to-month, and year-to-year). We even idolize people we perceive as being machine-like (like pro athletes). I've even seen messages, particularly in weight loss and exercise circles, that we need to be at war with our bodies and that we can bend them to our will if we have the right mindset. Did you hear that!? At war! Bending to our will! YIKES!

If paying attention to your body is not on your radar ... or maybe it *is* in your everyday life but not in your business ... you're not alone. Business culture is just a reflection of the dominant ideals in society. Listening to our bodies and befriending our nervous systems is a foreign concept. But, if we don't tune in, not only is there no space to create and cultivate joy, we can actually find all kinds of ways to lose it.

Like so many themes in this book, I could have written an entire book on the relationship between joy, your nervous system, and business (and perhaps I will someday). These next three conversations will help get you started tuning in.

WHEN YOUR BODY SAYS NO, BUT YOU STILL GO GO GO

I'm writing this conversation in March 2022. The Ukraine has been invaded by Russia in an unprovoked attack. Everything in my brain is telling me to stay the course — to keep working. I'm not watching the news. I'm recording this conversation in Otter.AI instead. But everything in my *body* is telling me, *take care of your emotional health right now, do things that are soothing, you don't need to be hitting arbitrary deadlines.*

This is a conversation I have with myself all the time, even though I know my joy seeps away when I insist on operating in a linear way, overriding the natural rhythms and flows of my body.

Most of us, at least in the United States, are indoctrinated into the 9-to-5, Monday-to-Friday work week. In the academic world I was raised in (both of my parents were professors) and then joined briefly as a PhD student, the indoctrination is even more extreme: There is no such thing as down time. "Publish or perish" means that working evenings, weekends, and all through breaks in classes is the norm. Summer was the time to catch up on work, not to rest.

After finishing my PhD, not working weekends at Facebook felt like a downshift from the hustle and grind I was accustomed to. Except that the norm there was to be on ALL the time Monday through Friday. I often started my workday when I jumped on a company shuttle from San Francisco to Menlo Park at 6:30 a.m. I'd close my computer when I jumped off the shuttle at the end of the day, sometimes at 7 p.m. or later, but I would often be drawn into Messenger conversations on my phone until bed.

The idea of "listening to my body" simply didn't exist in academia or the corporate world; at least not when I was there.

When I started my business, deprogramming from the 9-to-5 (and really the always-on mentality) was a struggle. There's a popular "sound" on TikTok that says "I didn't want to work a 9-to-

5, so now I work 24/7." Though I wasn't quite that extreme, I was joining the ranks of many entrepreneurs who struggle to turn off. As I set up my schedule, I didn't ask myself, "When am I at my best?" or "How can I build wiggle room into my schedule to account for life happenings or how my energy shifts day-to-day and week-to-week?" or even, "How many hours do I really need to be working in a week to accomplish my business and personal goals?" It's taken me several years of making small shifts to create a business that runs on the rhythms of my body. First I built a schedule around when I am most alert and productive. Then I got rid of most deadlines. Every deadline in my business is made up. I'll never wake up after missing a deadline to find that my business has fallen apart. I can always push things out by a few days, weeks, or sometimes months. And trying to stick to deadlines can prompt me to override my body's needs. (By the way, some people do very well with deadlines. I'm just not one of them!)

After making schedule and deadline changes, I dug deeper. I reconsidered my beliefs about what makes a "good" entrepreneur. I began unwinding the internalized capitalistic notion that my self-worth is tied to my productivity and abandoned the notion that productivity happens only in a linear way. I decided that there is nothing wrong with me when I have to take a day off because my anxiety has flared up. Or when I take long pauses on writing my book because my **creative** juices aren't flowing. Likewise, I came to understand that I'm not "less than" because I don't want to pack my schedule just to make more money and I work best going deep with only a handful of clients at a time. I had to let go of the notion that a valuable thought leader posts on Instagram every day. (My **creativity** comes in waves, and my posts do too.)

When I listen to my body and allow myself to follow the waves of my energy, my coaching is more masterful. My writing is more **creative**. I can do less but create more impact.

The same is likely true for you too — you've just been taught not to trust your body! Every creature on earth operates in cycles, including us. We have times of day that we're more energized and others when we're not. We go through seasons, lasting from days or weeks, to several months or years. People who menstruate literally go through a cycle every month that impacts everything from energy to **creativity** to mood.

How often are you ebbing and flowing with your cycles? Are you allowing yourself to be productive when your energy is high and rest when your energy is low? Are you attuned to the way your body ticks? Or are you trapped, like many people, in the beliefs that society has handed you about productivity?

Your joy depends on you listening to the rhythms of your body. And though it may feel uncomfortable as you begin to tune in, over time, I know you'll find yourself more productive and doing higher quality work.

GOING TO BATTLE AGAINST YOUR NERVOUS SYSTEM

Is your nervous system a friend that you lovingly attend to, or a foe that you try to defeat, override, or ignore?

If this question has you wondering what this has to do with joy in your business, read on. It's likely you've been paying too little attention to your nervous system, your body's command center that has influence over your automatic responses, thoughts, feelings, and actions. This is true for many of us whose success is derived from our intellectual abilities, as well as those who've been taught to ignore physical and emotional signals in favor of logic and reason. I like to call this "living from the neck up."

Most professional settings are over-rotated towards intellect, facts, logic, and reason. Emotions are a distraction at best, completely unwelcome at worst (since we're talking about societal systems, I should note this is a hallmark of white supremacy culture). The same focus tends to show up in business culture. Even the personal development world tends to be neck up, focusing on how to shift your mindset. A popular mantra in coaching is "Change your thoughts, change your life," and it is stated similarly in Cognitive Behavioral Therapy (a very thoughts-orientated treatment modality that can be helpful for some people in specific applications). There are certainly times when it makes sense to be in our heads — to lean on logic and reason, or focus on changing our thoughts. But if that was appropriate all the time, then we might as well be floating heads in jars (like in the cartoon Futurama) instead of full-bodied humans! There's so much more going on below our necks than we realize — and more than we allow ourselves to feel or tune into! In fact, there are more neurons in the rest of our bodies than in our brains. Science is only beginning to scratch the surface of understanding how our nervous systems work and how we can best listen to them.

Even if you haven't paid much attention to your nervous system in the past, you've certainly experienced it in action. Consider the scenario where you're on stage delivering a talk to a waiting crowd. Your palms might sweat. Your heart may race. As you begin to speak, your voice might sound jittery or even crack. That's all your nervous system reacting to what it perceives as a threat.

Whenever we face a threat — whether it's social like being laughed at or booed on stage, or physical like being followed down a dark alley — our bodies will respond in one of four ways: fight, flight, freeze, or fawn.

To illustrate how each of these 4 Fs can show up in your business, let's shift to another example. Not everyone speaks on stage, but most of us do engage in social media, whether for business or pleasure. Imagine you've made a post or video on your favorite platform and someone leaves an angry comment disagreeing with you.

If your nervous system goes into *fight*, you might "yell" at the person or insult them in a written response. Later, you might make a new post from an angry or defensive stance to pre-emptively deal with future antagonists or trolls.

In *flight*, you'll likely feel anxious or nervous, and have an urge to run and hide. You might delete the post, or if the flight urge is extreme, end up deleting your social media account altogether. If you do stay online, the next time you go to post, you might find yourself overthinking the post's photo and caption, hoping to be as inoffensive as possible.

In *freeze*, you might stare at your computer or phone, searching for something to say in response to the angry comment, but completely blank out.

And in *fawn*, you're likely to immediately apologize to the person for what you've said. You might even change your opinion to match theirs.

Your nervous system can also go into multiple modes. I used to go into a combination of flight and freeze on social media before learning how to recognize and soothe my nervous system's response. In all 4 Fs, your nervous system both responds in the moment, and also shapes your future actions in similar situations. The fear/threat response is a joy-suck that keeps on sucking, until you learn to be in tune with your nervous system.

Chances are your nervous system is in one of the 4 Fs in your business more often than you're aware. You may have been led to believe that you have a mindset block rather than a nervous system challenge. Maybe you've been told not to trust your nervous system, and that you should bypass what it's telling you.

Befriending your nervous system creates more space for joy.

By listening to our nervous systems (we'll cover one of those ways next in *Uncomfortable versus Unsafe*), we can learn when it's time for courage and when it's time to say no. And by having compassion for the ways our nervous system is trying to protect us, we can begin to work through fears, beliefs, and traumas that might be holding us back from activities and projects that will bring us a lot of joy. For instance, once I began to understand my nervous system's response to social media, I was able to self-soothe and self-coach, and courageously put myself out there more. It took a couple of years of coaching and therapy specifically geared at my nervous system — I had a lot to work through! — but now showing up on social media is more connective and joy-full than I ever imagined possible.

BEFRIENDING YOUR NERVOUS SYSTEM

Here's an exercise you can do when you feel stuck, afraid, anxious, or physically agitated. It will help you identify what is happening below the surface so you can come back to joy.

What is the circumstance? (Make this as neutral as possible. Example: Someone commented on my Instagram post that my opinion about the phrase "Change your thoughts, change your life" is wrong.)

What thoughts am I having about this circumstance? (Name the most prevalent thought. Example: I'm stupid and clearly am not suited to being a thought leader.)

What feeling am I having? (Name the most prevalent feeling. Example: shame.)

Where am I noticing this thought or feeling in or around my body? (Example: There's a lump in my throat. It feels like a steel ball clogging everything up.)

(Now focus all of your attention on that sensation. As you focus, begin to ask that sensation questions like it is another person sitting in a chair next to you. If this feels a little strange, I get it. I was a skeptic until I realized that I could learn a lot by talking to my body!)

Is there anything you want me to know about why you're here right now?

What are you afraid might happen to me? What are you protecting me from?

What do you need from me right now? Reassurance? For us to take a deep breath? A new thought or belief for us to try out?

In some cases, your system might ease or soften just by paying attention to it, allowing you to move forward. In others, it will ask you for soothing or deep breaths. And in others, it will say, "Hey, I need you to put on the brakes. Today is not the day to move forward." Honor whatever your system says it needs. Despite some of the popular rhetoric about our bodies being unreliable narrators, I personally believe they are wise well beyond what our conscious minds can comprehend.

UNCOMFORTABLE VERSUS UNSAFE
(WHEN TO LEAN INTO COURAGE AND WHEN TO LEAN OUT)

Being in business requires us to stretch and challenge ourselves. Joy requires that too. **Courage** comes into play here. If you spend any time reading personal development articles or hanging out in the company of self-help enthusiasts, chances are you'll come across mantras like "Feel the fear and do it anyway" and "FEAR = False Evidence Appearing Real." Interpreting these without a critical gaze can leave us feeling that all fear should be met with **courageous** action. I'd like to challenge that.

Yes, sometimes we need to feel the fear and do it anyway. Yes, sometimes we perceive a threat or danger that isn't actually there. Leaning into fear to get to what we desire on the other side of it can be immensely joy-full. But sometimes it's quite the opposite. Sometimes it creates misery. *Sometimes it even does harm.*

My therapist introduced me to a powerful distinction a couple of years ago: feeling uncomfortable versus feeling unsafe.

This distinction is not something that happens in our heads. Instead, it happens in our bodies. There might be something we want to do that cognitively, seems like it should be fine. We might tell ourselves our fear is just a fear, and that doing it anyway should be no big deal. And yet, our bodies might have a very different opinion.

During my first year in business, one of my coaches encouraged me to go live on Facebook for 90 days straight. The goal was for me to get comfortable sharing my thoughts and opinions more broadly than just with my clients and coach peers. At the time, I wasn't sure exactly what I had to offer that wasn't blatantly obvious or that others weren't already saying. In my coach's mind, there was no better way for me to find out than to hit "Go Live" and share whatever was top-of-mind, pouring it out stream-of-conscious style, each day. In principle, she was right. One of the best ways to get clarity on anything is to take messy action. And there's also something about speaking out loud that aids that clarity in a different way than writing.

My head was completely on board with the challenge. My friend, Inés, who you will meet in *Put on Your Lab Coat AND Feel Your Feelings Too*, once told me that the only way to know your message is to speak it over and over again. Her words continuously played in my mind. My body, on the other hand, was *not* on board. I was filled with dread. I had many Facebook Friends who had previously been my colleagues from when I worked there. I already had mind drama about what those folks thought of me leaving tech to become a coach, and now I was going to talk about coaching with them!!??? SHIT. I also had Facebook Friends that met me during my academic life, including several members of the PhD committee that evaluated my dissertation and greenlit me to be called Dr. ... Hoo'boy! What were *they* going to think of me? First I left academia for Facebook, and now I'd left that to become a coach!!?? What if I shared my social psychology knowledge wrong? What if I shared things that were pseudoscience or spiritual garbage? Would they consider me a disgrace to the academy? Would they think I didn't deserve my PhD?

Those fears were just scratching the surface of what was happening internally. Deeper down, I was worried about showing up in people's News Feeds *every day*. Back then, that was way outside the norm, at least on my feed. *I'll be taking up too much space. People will think I'm too much. They'll think I'm arrogant or egotistical. I'm going to lose people from my life.*

But in an effort to "feel the fear and do it anyway," and also to avoid showing my coach any weakness, I convinced myself that I *had* to do the challenge. I brought my head back into the equation as a cheerleader, reminding myself that I wanted to be more visible, and that action would indeed create clarity.

The first few days of the challenge were brutal. I had a panic attack every day either before or after I went live. Sometimes both before *and* after. I'd burst into tears and my whole body would shake. One of those days I curled up in a ball, writhing on the floor because there was so much energy going through me. All the while, I kept telling myself that I needed to push through. That this challenge was not a big deal. I never once considered reaching out to my coach to tell her what was going on. I was mortified that she'd lose all respect for me if she found out what a scaredy-cat I was.

In essence, I was shaming myself and my body for its response to being visible on social media. I carried that shame until I offhandedly shared about the Facebook Live challenge with my therapist, an expert in Somatic Experiencing (a body-based therapeutic modality), a couple years later. That's when she shared the distinction about feeling uncomfortable versus unsafe.

She confirmed that when your nervous system feels uncomfortable, that's not necessarily a sign to slow down or put on the brakes. In fact, it may be a sign that you are heading in the right direction of growth or learning. In those circumstances, it makes sense to, as Brené Brown says, "Choose courage over comfort." However, she went on to explain that if your nervous system feels unsafe, it's having a trauma response. Continuing to push through anyway is overriding that trauma response and *potentially creating even more trauma*.

The tricky thing about feeling uncomfortable versus unsafe is that we can't always be sure of the difference. Remember, our conscious minds are good at telling us stories about what is and isn't dangerous. In my Facebook Live challenge, my mind thought everything was safe. Even if I had known the distinction, my mind might have convinced me that what I was feeling was uncomfortable. But the fact that I was having daily panic attacks to the point of being curled up on the floor says otherwise. Was my body responding to all the fears I was consciously aware of? Fears of being judged by my Facebook colleagues or academic mentors? Fears around taking up space and being seen as arrogant? I don't know.

> We can't always determine
> what our body is responding to.
> But we can know that our body is telling us to stop.

And we can honor that signal without judging or shaming it. However, that action doesn't have to feel unsafe forever. We can dial back whatever we're doing to find actions that *are* safe, even if still a bit uncomfortable, as we build up tolerance toward doing the original action. For me, that might have been sending videos to a handful of trusted friends and colleagues every day rather than blasting my entire Facebook feed. We can heal the beliefs and traumas that are causing our nervous system's alarm bells to go off in the safety of therapy or a trauma-informed or trauma-trained coach.

(Note: trauma-informed or trauma-trained is important here. Coaches can unintentionally do more harm than good if they don't have proper knowledge and training.)

So, as you take courageous action, be sure to check in with your nervous system. If you feel a bit uncomfortable, lean in. But if any part of you feels unsafe at any point, lean out.

There's no shame in getting in motion thinking it's a little uncomfortable and then realizing, "Nope, this is unsafe," and pumping the brakes. As soon as you know that, look for another route to where you want to go or find a way to dial back the extremity on the route you are taking. And seek support! Every bit of healing you do makes more space for joy!

FOCUS ON THE PRESENT ... BUT NOT *TOO* MUCH

Hold on to your socks ... I'm about to say something sacrilegious: Focusing on the present can steal your joy.

I know, I know. Didn't I tell you to let go of future-focus in *Goal Trap #3 – Chasing Happiness* in favor of experiencing joy now? And what about all the articles and Instagram-perfect quotes and memes that tell us how much future-tripping and past-dwelling is stealing our joy?? Heck, didn't the Buddha say, "Do not dwell on the past, do not dream of the future, concentrate the mind on the present moment"? To a large extent, what I said is true. As is the wisdom of Instagram, and of course, the Buddha. But it's also overly simplified.

We need the past, present, *and* future to thrive. Nothing's all bad, and nothing's all good. Sure we can get trapped in the past, but there are also psychological benefits of nostalgia — including increasing our optimism and deepening our sense of connectedness. And sure, we can spend so much time planning for and thinking about the future (which we often hope will be better than today) that we're missing out on the joy of the present. But thinking about our future selves also helps us to do healthy things like plan for retirement and pursue long-term dreams and goals. Assuming long-term goals are a joy-full pursuit for you (see *"How Monsters", Inner Critics, and the Killjoys of Long-Term Goals*). There are lots of psychological and nervous system benefits of being focused on the here and the now ... but it can also make us short-sighted.

In business, we often want results ... now. We want cash flow, revenue, great clients ... now. We want to know if an action, activity, or project is going to be a success or failure ... now. If we're overly focused on now, we can forget that business is a long game. Not every seed that gets planted will grow into something right away, or at all. (We'll talk more in-depth about this in a later conversation called *Fe-Fi-Fo-Fum ... Plant Some Magic Beans*.) Not every goal we set can be worked toward or achieved in the short-term.

> When we expand our mental horizons
> beyond the here and now,
> we can *create more* joy in the here and now.

And technically we can double dip, experiencing joy now and again when something comes to fruition in the future. Before we talk about expanding our mental horizons, let's explore how overly focusing on the present can steal our joy.

When we are focused on immediate results, we only take actions that we believe will produce them. For instance, when I was first building my business, the only local meetups I would attend were ones that I thought would be an opportunity to meet potential clients. If I didn't have a business-based reason to attend something, I wouldn't. I felt like I didn't have time to be playing around with meetups that wouldn't pay-off in the short-term. But that meant I wasn't looking for meetups that would fill my joy tank. I'm curious now about how much I missed out on because I had my blinders on. I was trapped in thinking about what "I should" go to. And I'm sure that my energy at those events was off too. Nobody is attracted to someone who clearly has an agenda to find clients, even when it's an energetic, rather than spoken, agenda.

We also tend to worry more about short-term failures when we are overly present-focused. If we're not seeing our business as a long game, any failures we experience in the here and the now feel like a much bigger deal. We might even see them as a sign we should give up or quit.

So why do we get trapped in the here and now in our businesses? Besides the messaging that pedestalizes present-focused thinking, we also feel like the present is more certain and controllable than the future. We have to trust and surrender to the unknown if we take actions or do activities that have an indefinite timeline for results. That can feel *wildly* uncomfortable.

Now, I'm not saying that you need to shift completely away from present-focus. In fact, we can be both present and future-focused at the same time, creating joy in the here and the now, as well as potentially in the future.

There will be times when immediate results are necessary. Not every business has the privilege of going months without revenue or cash flow. When you need cash, focus on that! But you can also expand your horizons for the future by choosing more joy in the present. That is, including in your overall strategy any actions, activities, and projects that bring you joy right now and also might help you on the path toward longer term goals ... or turn into interesting opportunities in the future.

In early 2022, I hosted a Magic Bean party, purely for my own joy, on Zoom. (You don't need to have read *Fe-Fi-Fo-Fum ... Plant Some Magic Beans* to get this example). I shared it in my newsletter and posted about it several times on Instagram. My friend, Michelle, saw all my posts, but only decided to say, "Hey, send me the link. I'll be there," hours before the event. Afterwards, she messaged me to say that she had talked herself out of coming for days. In her words, she didn't have a business case to attend. It was only hours before the call that she realized, "Wait, 'because I want to' is business case enough!" She had a lovely time and even connected with a new friend or two. Will those turn into anything business-related down the road? Who knows. I know that at least one new person follows her on Instagram now and loves her content. The joy of connection was energizing and bled over into other activities Michelle did in the coming days. Whether she can see it (or ever will see it) chances are, filling up her joy tank helped her business.

Where might you be keeping out joy by only doing what you believe will either pay off right away or stave off failure?

What are some steps you can take to allow a bit of future-focus to guide your actions and activities?

Where can you decide that joy is a business case enough?

CUTTING OFF, EXILING, OR STUFFING DOWN "PARTS" OF YOU THAT "DON'T BELONG IN BUSINESS"

We are multifaceted humans. We contain a multitude of "parts" — thoughts, emotions, beliefs, qualities and characteristics, personality traits, identities and roles that make up who we are. If you've ever said, "A part of me feels X, but another part of me feels Y", you're already somewhat familiar with this concept.

We all have certain parts of ourselves that we deem "good" or acceptable — these are parts of us that we believe are allowed in any context. One of my "good" parts is my highly intellectual part. I see it as beneficial to my success, so I allow it to show up in my business, relationships, hobbies, and even my alone time. That intellectual part is always welcome to the party. Another part that I welcome no matter the context is my loving part (for obvious reasons 😊).

We also all have parts of ourselves that we deem "bad" or unacceptable. These are parts of us that we try to suppress or get rid of. I have an anxious part that can take me out for an entire day, and a shy part that sometimes stops me from putting my message out into the world. If I could only find a way to bury them for good …

And then there's a middle ground where some parts are welcome in certain contexts or situations, but not in others. A part of me loves to rap at karaoke. Warren G, Coolio, and Eminem are my specialities. I love to perform, and sometimes relish in the attention I get when I'm being silly. That part was not always welcome in my professional world. In fact, I was mortified at the possibility that my PhD advisor would find out I did karaoke every Friday during grad school because I didn't want him to think that part of me existed.

Our beliefs about which parts are always good, always bad, or acceptable in certain contexts but not in others, rarely come from within us. Sometimes we've inferred a message from the media or society at large, like what being a professional looks and feels like. Sometimes, we've been explicitly told by parents, teachers, friends, or mentors what is and isn't allowable. Perhaps a part of you emerged when you were young, but someone told you to put it back in the proverbial box. Or it came out in a situation where it wasn't all that useful and you decided to stuff it away completely. It only takes one instance of being told a part of you is wrong or seeing that a part of you is incompatible with a situation for you to extrapolate and decide it's unacceptable to everyone and in all situations.

In our businesses, we tend to allow only a limited range of parts of ourselves to come to the table. But, it's unlikely that those parts are the only ones that can help us be successful. You likely have parts that you're actively suppressing because you see them as detrimental to your business, but they'd be surprisingly beneficial to bring out. Until you experiment with ones that feel safe to try, you won't know. You're just operating on an untested belief.

One of my clients was known as a free spirit from a very young age. Her free spirit part took her on all kinds of wild adventures in her teens and twenties. But when she began to build a name for herself in corporate — and then considered stepping out into entrepreneurship — she tried to keep that free spirit part as buried as possible. She was worried that if any little piece of her free spirit got out, people wouldn't respect her or see her as professional. But, keeping her free spirit locked away also meant that she was burying some **creativity** and spontaneity that could make her work more impactful. So we explored how her free spirit could have a naturally valuable role in her work and then slowly experimented with bringing it out and seeing the results. She was promoted and took on a much larger role in the organization just a few months later. Was it because of her free spirit part? We can't know. But what we do know is that her work was much more joy-full with her free spirit welcome at the table.

CUTTING OFF "PARTS" OF YOU THAT "DON'T BELONG IN BUSINESS"

In the spirit of my client's free spirit, let's go back and visit my karaoke rapper part. Could it have a natural role in my business? Absolutely! We live in the TikTok and Instagram Reel era. People crave edutainment. Social media is the perfect playground for my karaoke rapper to have a little fun on occasion. I don't foresee myself going down the route of becoming a full-blown video content creator, but when I need a little creative spark or want to delight myself, my karaoke rapper is ready to play.

Now just because I've welcomed in my karaoke rapper and my client welcomed in her free spirit, doesn't mean that you need to welcome in every part of you to your business. And it doesn't mean that every welcome part needs to always be present. It's natural and healthy for parts to show up when they are useful; the key is to learn to leverage them when they are beneficial and letting them step aside when they aren't.

PARTS CHECK-IN

What parts of you are you holding down like a kick-board under water?

How is holding those parts down contributing to or draining your joy?

Which parts could you get **curious** about bringing back in?

How can you playfully experiment and explore what kind of role they might play for you in your business?

~~LOVE~~ JOY AND BASKETBALL

If you ask anyone who knew me growing up, they'd say that I was born with a basketball in my hand. I have no clue where my love of the sport came from. It certainly wasn't my parents. They never played, and to my knowledge, they didn't watch sports on TV. One of my earliest memories is of the 10-foot basketball hoop in the courtyard at my preschool. While everyone else was riding tricycles around the courtyard, I wanted to be throwing a ball at that hoop.

Maybe the mere presence of a hoop at my preschool made enough of an impression on young me to inspire my love for the game, but part of me believes I was born with it. Growing up, Michael Jordan was my hero. I watched all six of the Bulls' NBA titles. I watched the original Dream Team win the gold medal at the Barcelona Olympics in 1992. Though I couldn't have a hoop in my driveway, I had a mini-hoop that hung off my bedroom closet door. I loved jumping from my bed for a slam dunk, mimicking Jordan's form, even down to his signature tongue hanging out. In my parents' building at the University of Arizona, I turned every recycling bin I could find into a basketball hoop until they got a mini-hoop (like the one in my bedroom) for their department's lounge.

When I joined my first youth basketball league in 3rd grade (the earliest I was allowed to participate by the Powers-That-Be), I was the only girl ("girl" because that's how I was gendered growing up, though now identify as nonbinary). None of the boys liked that a girl was playing with them. Several of them, including the coaches' sons, teased me mercilessly. But I didn't care. My love of basketball was too strong. Throughout elementary school, I joined enough leagues and programs to be playing basketball multiple days of the week. Sometimes it was every day but Sunday. Basketball was all I thought about. It was all I wanted to do.

In middle school, I went to every summer basketball camp I could. Overnight camps at University of Arizona, University of Michigan, and Michigan State University. Day camps at various places in northern Michigan. As I got exposed to other girls playing basketball, I realized that I was pretty good. I can't tell you that I was the best player to ever walk the earth, but I was good enough to make the "All Star Team" at all the overnight camps. When I was finally eligible to join the middle school basketball team in 7th grade, I was the only non-8th grader on the A team (we had A, B, and C teams). I was also one of the best players on the team, if not the best. The same was true the next year. I knew the likelihood of playing college basketball was slim, but I thought I just might have a shot.

Everything changed my freshman year of high school.

Most of my life, I played a position called shooting guard, which, if you're not familiar with basketball, means that I played far away from the basket. I had a good shot and a long range. I wasn't always the tallest player. I also wasn't the strongest. I was 110 pounds and could barely bench press the bar. So I wasn't fit to play positions like center or power forward that were almost always for the tallest and strongest players. But somehow, when I got to freshman year of high school, I was taller than all the other girls my age. I hadn't grown. All the older girls on the JV and varsity team (many of whom I'd played with on the A team in middle school) were still taller than me. But the freshman girls were unusually short as a group, and among them, I was a tower.

So, my freshman team coach, Coach Flores, deciding entirely based on my height, moved me out of my natural role of shooting guard to center. I was devastated. I didn't want to play center. I loved shooting from far out. I loved trying to figure out how to be quicker than my defender, even though I wasn't the quickest person. I loved being able to run around the whole court. The center's job was to stay near the basket and bully people around them to score. It wasn't fun for me at all. Despite this, when we played other schools, I was decently successful at center, scoring a handful of points every game. When our team scrimmaged against the JV and Varsity teams, I got beat up. I pled with Coach Flores to move me back to shooting guard, but he wouldn't do it.

Moving out of my natural position wasn't the only thing that changed everything my freshman year. My parents took me to New York City for a conference and family holiday during Thanksgiving week, just as basketball season was getting into gear. The trip had been planned for months, but it turned out I missed two or three practices. As "punishment" for missing practices, I both lost my starting spot as center *and* had to sit out a game completely when I got back. Frustratingly, I was never able to earn my starting spot back or Coach Flores' trust. In his mind, I wasn't dedicated enough. And though I never missed another practice that season, he continually searched for evidence of my lack of dedication. I wasn't the fastest runner on the team. To Flores, I was lazy. I wasn't the strongest on the team. To Flores, I didn't push myself hard enough. No matter how much I tried to get back in his good graces, he found ways to tell me that I just wasn't as good at basketball as I thought.

Any gains I'd made with Flores during the season were wiped out when summer rolled around. My family spent every summer at a cottage in Michigan (we primarily lived in Arizona). So I wasn't around in the summer to participate in unofficial, non-mandatory summer practices and open gyms. That wasn't okay with Coach Flores. I thought I made a fair compromise by staying in Tucson the first few weeks of summer to attend some of the most important events. My parents had already left for Michigan and at 15 without a driver's license, I stayed with a friend and her parents transported me to all things basketball. Me staying back for a few weeks wasn't enough for Flores, though. The fact that I was going to Michigan to be with my family at all was, according to him, evidence that I didn't really care enough about basketball.

The message was loud and clear: If I wanted to play this sport that I loved more than anything ... that I ate, slept and breathed from the time I was a toddler ... I needed to forfeit the position I was strongest at, and play one that I didn't love. I also had to give up going to Michigan in the summers. Which meant giving up family *and also* summer camp — which was the only place I truly felt safe and welcome at the time. And as if it couldn't get any more crushing, the message was laced with, "you're just not as good as you think you are."

It would have been one thing if Coach Flores had been coming from a place of, "You're really talented and have potential to play in college, but this is the reality of what it takes to do so. And I'm here to support you every step of the way." Though it would have been difficult, I imagine I would have been all-in on that. But instead it was coming from, "You don't have what it takes."

At the beginning of sophomore year, I made the excruciating decision to quit basketball. I gave up my first love in favor of summer camp, family, time at the cottage, and really, not feeling like crap all the time.

I thought I'd never find anything I loved as much as basketball … and then I found coaching.

Why am I telling this story in a book on joy in business? Because that story became *the story* for me. When I started my coaching business, what I was told about basketball became what I believed about my coaching and my business:

Your strengths and genius don't matter. If you want to be successful, you'll have to play how you're told to, not how you want to.

You'll have to make sacrifices. If you're not fully dedicated **at all costs***, then why are you wasting time going for it at all?*

Don't even believe that you're good at what you do. You're **never** *as good as you think you are.*

It wasn't just basketball that led to the self-doubt and not-enoughness I carried into coaching and my business. The narrative that started in basketball was reinforced several times over the

~~LOVE~~ JOY AND BASKETBALL

next few decades. One of those times was in my PhD program. My advisor specialized in a theoretical framework I wasn't thrilled about, but I was excited to work with him because of what research questions he was applying the framework to. Unfortunately, it turned out that he had no intention of helping me find what I was naturally interested in or curious about. So I spent four years being told that if I wanted to play this game called "academic job", I needed to give up my natural curiosities and strengths. Hell, I was so busy doing his research that I didn't have the time and space to even discover what they were. (Spoiler alert: that was one of *many* reasons I didn't go down the academic path.)

Early in my time at Facebook, my beliefs about who I needed to be in order to be successful were reinforced again. I was hired as a Quantitative User Experience Researcher because of my expertise in running surveys and analyzing data. But the department I was placed in when I arrived at Facebook didn't know what to do with me. Most of the teams that I was supposed to provide research support for hadn't been exposed to much quantitative research before. The qualitative researchers, who did more interview-based work, were each assigned to a specific team of product managers, engineers, and designers to work with, but I was supposed to float around and work with different teams as needed. That model didn't work well at all. I wasn't embedded enough in the teams to know what decisions they were making that could be supported by a survey or data analysis. They also didn't know enough about quantitative research to reach out for my support. I confided in my manager that I felt lost. I didn't have many projects to work on and I wasn't sure what my role was. She assured me all was okay.

Around that same time, my dad passed away suddenly. I took an emergency flight home to Arizona to deal with some legal issues quickly. As an only child to divorced parents, I was the executor of the estate. It took me several weeks of work time to sort through everything. At the same time, my house in San Francisco flooded. (I don't know how that happens while living on a hill in San Francisco, but sure enough, it did!) My then-wife, our pets, and I were displaced from our house for over a week, and the repairs took much longer. So for the first six or eight months of my Facebook career, I was not being used for my natural skills and abilities while also dealing with grief, legal issues, and a disrupted home life. I would have worried about my performance review, except that my manager assured me all was well.

So, naturally, I was shocked when I sat down for my first performance review and my manager said, "Erin you got a 'Meets *Most* Expectations' and you're going on a Performance Improvement Plan (PIP). We even took into account that your dad died." If you're not familiar with corporate speak, a PIP is often a "Get in shape or we'll tell you get out" warning. She went on to tell me, just like Coach Flores, all the ways in which I wasn't as good as I thought I was. Apparently, in my anxiety to find a role for myself I had said things to colleagues that came off as dismissive of qualitative research. But rather than being given a chance to fix the damage directly with my colleagues shortly after it happened, I wasn't even aware there was damage until it was on my record.

As part of trying to save my job during the PIP, I gave up my "natural position" — quantitative research — and learned qualitative research. I also learned, like I did in basketball, to put my family priorities last. I was able to stay at Facebook and become successful over the next few years, including moving into management, but thanks to the message from my first manager, I never allowed myself to think I was good at what I did.

Fast forward to 2018 when I started my business. The beliefs that started in basketball and had become more ingrained over the years, were running the show now, but I wasn't conscious of them just yet.

I'd become a basketball center, construal-level theorist, and qualitative researcher ... what was the "giving up my natural position" equivalent going to be in my business?

I'd started my business partially to spend time with family and have more space for hobbies ... running through my head were questions like "How soon would I have to admit to myself that to be truly successful I was going to have to put my business above all else?", "How could I make sure that I never ever got to a point of believing that I was good at what I do?" and "How could I ensure I stayed in a perpetual state of feeling not enough so that I'd never have to hear, 'You're not as good as you think you are' from anyone ever again?"

Recall from *Joy is Uncomfortable* that we experience joy when we are in our Zone of Genius. Starting with being moved to center from shooting guard in high school, I got message after message that if I wanted to keep doing what I loved (basketball, psychology, research at Facebook), that I needed to give up my Zone of Genius. So of course, I didn't even consider what my natural strengths and geniuses were. I looked around at other people to see who I was supposed to be and what I was supposed to do. I also listened to people who were eager to give me their opinions on who I should be and what I should do. Not a recipe for joy!

I got message after message that I wasn't dedicated enough and that I wasn't as good at what I was doing as I had thought … that led to me working too hard and coming from a place of harsh self-criticism and desperation to prove myself. Also not a recipe for joy!

The beliefs that were instilled in me from my childhood, and got reinforced throughout my adulthood, were keeping me from my joy as I leapt into business. It took me years of growth work through coaching and therapy to make the connection between my experience in basketball and how I show up in my business. Now anytime I see a belief driving the bus in my business, I try to find the source and re-write the narrative from older, hopefully wiser, me.

What are some of the core stories and beliefs that you hold? They may be ones that have been with you so long that you've just accepted them as true or they may have come from life-shaping events.

Which of them are keeping you from stepping fully into who you are and doing what's most joy-full?

How long have you been carrying them with you?

Are they true? If yes, can you be *absolutely sure* they are true? If not, what new beliefs do you want to try on instead?

How can following joy become a compass for rewriting those beliefs?

How the F*ck Do We Get More Joy?

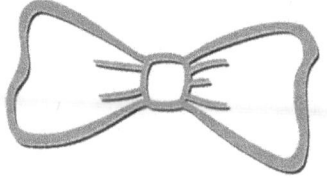

How The F*ck Do We Get More Joy?

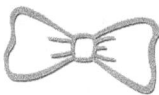

Let's go back to one of the distinguishing features of joy: It's a resource that comes from within us. We always have access to it, and we can also create and cultivate more of it over time.

I picture us all having a joy tank. From that lens, the previous section of the book was about ways joy seeps, leaks, and drains from our tank (as well as what we can do to plug those seeps and leaks or prevent the drain to begin with). If your only focus moving forward is preventing joy from seeping away, you still can have a joy-full business. But I suspect you're here to be joy-full *AF*. Putting joy first is not just about "not losing" joy, it's about filling up on as much of it as possible, and even expanding your capacity for it.

As we talked about in *But Joy Is*, joy is the key to long-term, sustainable business success. When we have delight, play, creativity, and/or connection to ourselves and something deeper, we are more likely to stay in for the long haul. But those positives are not the only reason we need to stay filled up on joy.

> *"Joy collected over time fuels resilience – ensuring we'll have reservoirs of strength when hard things do happen."*
>
> ~ Brené Brown

Entrepreneurship requires incredible resilience. We don't have the same level of certainty that someone working a traditional 9-to-5 corporate job might have. (Though how certain is anything really when employers can lay off or fire people at a moment's notice?) We will inevitably go through long periods of time when nothing is working or our revenue dips. Depending on our business, we might be more susceptible to economic downturns or changing consumer preferences. Whether or not we have others to lead in our businesses, we must lead ourselves. That means getting cozy with our fears and doubts, learning what we struggle with and need outside help on, managing failure, and championing ourselves to move forward even when everything feels too hard and overwhelming. The more joy we have, the more able we are to weather any storm.

Joy is also an act of resistance.

Throughout this book, I've mentioned several societal influences on what we pursue and how (patriarchy, white supremacy, toxic capitalism, individualism). Being in our joy, and truly being in our fully authentic selves, is a way to break away from these oppressive systems. I believe that the more of us break away, the more we'll begin to break down systems and make room for positive social change.

Whether you purely want more joy for the joy of it, like the idea of creating fuel for resilience, or are ready to smash the patriarchy (and more), this section has something for you. Some conversations will help you find ways to infuse joy into everything you do (like … *AND it's Joy-full (Baking Joy into Every Goal)* and *Fill Up Your Joy Tank*). Others will give you specific suggestions (like *Fe-Fi-Fo-*

Fum ... Plant Some Magic Beans and *It's All Fun and Games ... No, Really!*) Feel free to pick and choose what works for you. (After all, if I haven't said it enough already, your way is always the most joy-full way.)

... AND IT'S JOY-FULL (BAKING JOY INTO EVERY GOAL)

When I say that creating and cultivating joy is an essential business strategy, I'm not saying that it should be your *only* strategy. I don't think it can be. But I do think it can inform all your other strategies in terms of what you pursue and how.

I also don't think being joy-full can be your only goal. In fact, it doesn't work well as a stand-alone. Goals are often specific, quantifiable targets that we move towards. We can measure our progress towards them, and assess where we might need to adjust or pivot in order to move forward. Once we hit our target, we often set a new one. Though we can always want more joy, there is no quantifiable target amount of joy-fullness to move towards. We can sort of measure progress, but it's more difficult to understand how far we need to go. That's because there is no "there" to get to — we can be "full" of joy, but there is infinite room for more. So once we start feeling joy-full, we can't just say "great, I checked that goal off the list. What's next?"

Joy-fullness is an ongoing pursuit.

So of course it's important to have other goals in your business. (And I'm guessing you already have plenty of them.) You might have a revenue target, or maybe a number of clients or customers that you'd like to serve. If you're building a community or an app, you might have a specific amount of people you'd like to see actively engaged daily, weekly, and/or monthly. Or you might have a goal around retaining members of that community or app. You may have a creative project that you want to get out in the world, like I did with this book.

Where does joy fit when we're setting goals?

Let's play with the example of setting a revenue target. It's a goal that nearly every business owner sets at some point in time. For imagination's sake, let's say you want to make $200K in your business this year. What immediately comes to mind for you as you begin to think about going towards that goal? Do you jump to working through how many clients or customers you'll need to serve to hit that target? Do you dive into creative brainstorming of marketing ideas or programs/products you might need to offer?

How does it *feel* to think about going after a $200K goal? How many of the ideas that popped into your head are exciting and challenging? How many are things that you believe *should* work, or even have worked in the past, but don't light you up? How many actively make you miserable just thinking about them?

If going after $200K in revenue feels the opposite of joy-full to go after, or has the potential to turn that way, why not infuse joy into the goal at the outset?

What I mean by that is adding an "AND" — look! my favorite word! — to your goal: "I'm going to make $200K in my business this year AND it will be joy-full."

By putting an AND in the goal, you've created some parameters or constraints that weren't there before. In this case, they are a good thing. Because now you have to get curious and creative. What are the joy-full paths to creating $200K? What aren't? How can you ensure that you stay on the joy-full path, especially when other paths feel more certain to help you reach your goal? You might also need to take courageous action, knowing that some of the joy-full paths involve taking risks and/or trying things you've never done before. And you might need to have the courage to let go of tried-and-true ways of creating revenue that have felt meh or miserable in the past.

Adding "… AND it's joy-full" to your goals completely shifts the emotional, mental, and physical energy of pursuing them. *This is how joy as a strategy gets baked into everything you do.*

Exercise

Take stock of all of your current goals. You may want to revisit ones you already explored in the "Goal Traps Check-in" in *Falling Into All Four Traps*.

Which ones are you already pursuing joy-fully? What, if anything, needs to happen to keep the joy flowing?

Which are actively stealing your joy and how?

Which are going fine, but could use an extra joy infusion? What would make them more joy-full?

WHEN DO YOU FEEL JOY-FULL?

When do you feel joy-full AF in your business? Stop for a second and think.

Have you ever asked yourself this question? If the answer is no, I would venture to guess that even though you started your business wanting more joy (whether you called it that or not), it's never been an explicit goal. (And as we've discussed in multiple conversations, you're not alone in that.) Up until reading this book, I'd bet you've never actively sought to create or cultivate it in your business. And you've likely never checked in on your joy the way you might with other metrics in your business.

And even if you *have* asked yourself this question, perhaps it's time to check in and re-evaluate.

So whether you've asked yourself before or not, take some time to check in right now. *Don't flip to the next conversation. Do not pass go. Do not collect $200. Really pause and sit with your answers here.*

> When am I joy-full in my business?
> What am I doing?
> How am I doing it?
> Who am I with?

I am joy-full when I'm coaching my clients. Even when we are dealing with heavy topics like unresolved trauma or systemic oppression. (Yes, these both show up in business and are important contexts to work with.) My whole body is on fire as I work with the human sitting in front of me (whether in person or on my Zoom screen). Who is this person? What are they all about? What lights them up? How does their brain work? Where do they want to go and who do they want to become in the process of getting there?

I am also joy-full when I'm teaching other coaches about coaching. There's coaching that helps on the surface, leading to temporary changes or incremental improvements, and there's deep coaching that changes people at a cellular level. I'm passionate about helping coaches master the art and science of deep coaching, and helping them become more trauma, nervous-system, neurodiversity, and systems-of-oppression informed. Anytime I am mentoring or teaching another coach, I feel tapped into my **curiosity** and **creativity**, and feel more **connected** to the "collective".

You will likely find that certain activities bring you joy, just like coaching, teaching, and mentoring do for me. You may also find that certain *ways* you approach activities bring you joy. For instance, I feel joy-full when I have a big goal in front of me and low attachment to whether I reach it. (We'll talk about this more in *Put on your HILA Hat*.) When I don't know if or when I'll get to a destination, I can be more **curious** and **creative** about my path along the way, and I tend to take more risks because I'm not taking failure too seriously. I also feel joy-full when I turn activities I that don't inherently love doing into games (We'll dive into this in *It's All Fun and Games … No, Really!*).

A less obvious, but important source of your joy might be in partnering with your brain. That is, working with its natural function. I am someone who cannot create a masterpiece from a blank canvas. I need ideas to react to. I need someone to say, "what if you painted the emotion you are feeling right now?" or "draw me your best representation of a farm." I don't consider myself an artist, but the metaphor works well for me. In business terms, I need something concrete to grasp onto. If I'm writing content — for this book, my newsletter, or social media — I am best if I'm responding to something that has come up in a coaching call, conversation with a friend, book, or someone else's social media post. Without something to react to, my brain spins. It's like I'm swimming in an ocean of possible things to write about but I can't seem to find a single coral reef to focus on. Having something to react to or that triggers a thought (or series of thoughts) creates ease, and when I feel ease, I also feel more joy.

Back to checking on when you feel joy-full. As you reflect, scan for activities, people, circumstances, thoughts, and ways you partner with your brain. If you'd like to get an even deeper pulse on your joy, ask yourself what about them makes them feel joy-full. Then, feel free to do the opposite and look at when you are least joy-full.

If you'd prefer to reflect through a more formal exercise, you could draw a line down a piece of paper and write joy-full at the top of the left column and joy-less at the top of the right. For a week, any time you notice something that brings or steals your joy, write it in the appropriate column. Or if you'd like something even more structured, you can go back and revisit *Joy Audit*.

WHAT MAKES YOU COME ALIVE?

So … maybe you read the last conversation about what makes you most joy-full and immediately had all the answers. Or maybe you read the earlier conversations about your Zone of Genius and knew immediately what activities have you operating joy-fully in that zone. But maybe the Zone of Genius concept threw everything you knew about yourself on its head. Maybe you've been so steeped in (and rewarded for) your Zone of Excellence that you're not even sure where to begin looking for your Zone of Genius. [If this is you, you're not alone. A few years ago, I discovered one of my geniuses is helping people find their Zone of Genius. I did several coaching sessions with colleagues who were at the top of their games and had done a lot of previous self-development work. They all were completely blind to their geniuses.]

One of the best ways to load up on more joy is through the activities that make you feel most alive. Are you creating or building something? Researching or experimenting? Leading other people? Teaching or mentoring? Creating order from chaos? Of course, in business, we wear multiple hats — especially if we're solopreneurs or lead a small team — so I'm not asking which hats you wear. I'm asking which ones are you wearing when you feel alive? When do you feel most driven or energized? Remember, your Zone of Genius is what you're good at and what you love to do. So, looking at what you're naturally driven towards can give you a clue, at least to the part of "what you love to do." Chances are, because it's a natural driver for you, you're also good at it.

If you're still not sure what makes you come alive, look back to your childhood for clues. What were you most drawn to then? Did you love to play with LEGO® or building blocks? Perhaps you're a builder. Did you have a science kit? Perhaps you're a researcher. Were you constantly gathering your friends for adventures in treehouses, on playgrounds, or through neighborhoods? Perhaps you're a leader. Or were you, like me, the confidant and advisor for all of your friends?

I'd be willing to bet that whatever you do in business taps into your natural drivers, though perhaps you've not been aware of them up until now. Or maybe you have been aware of these drivers but have told yourself they have no place in your business.

One of my clients, Sami, was a VP at a global consulting company when she first started working with me. She knew that eventually, she wanted to move on to another career, possibly in entrepreneurship, but she wasn't sure what made her come alive. We had talked extensively about her creative side. Growing up she'd been an artist and in her spare time outside of her VP role, she had created a calendar company as a side hustle. But it wasn't until we dug into what she was doing in her VP role that she connected the dots — she was a builder. She'd been building a digital product from the ground up and she loved it. Once she realized that, she knew she didn't want to leave the company until she saw that product all the way through to launch. Even if there were parts of her job burning her out, building the product made her come so alive that she couldn't imagine leaving quite yet. When she did leave the company, and we began to explore what was next for her, we kept the "Sami is a builder" idea in mind, knowing that her joy depended on her being able to create a product or service from scratch. (As of this writing she is still in exploration or I'd tell you what she landed on!)

Another client, Cody, had been a teacher when we first started working together. They were pondering moving into another career, and like Sami, were intrigued by entrepreneurship. When we dug into Cody's natural drivers, we found out that they come alive when teaching, coaching, and advocating for people. Learning that opened up a world of possibility to Cody. They went on to complete a yoga teacher training and have since explored various ways they can combine their love of yoga and mindfulness with their love of being around and teaching young kids.

The more you can align your work to what naturally makes you come alive, the more joy-full you will be. Though I'm generally not a fan of "personality tests", one that might be helpful in exploring your natural drivers is the Sparketype Assessment created by Jonathan Fields.[11] As a researcher, I'm pretty critical of tests, so I have to say that I can't tell from how the methodology is described whether it's scientifically valid. In truth, most tests like these (like the Myers Briggs Type Indicator) look scientific, but aren't. I also can't say whether it covers the full range of natural drivers in existence. However, I do know it can be a useful lens. The assessment asks questions about your past and present. You then get information on which of the ten Sparketypes is your primary driver, which is secondary and helps support you in your primary driver, and which is your anti-driver — the activity that sucks your joy the most and you should avoid or outsource at all costs. I highly recommend taking the test, but I also recommend reading about all ten Sparketypes. Sometimes you don't need an assessment to know what feels intuitively true for you.

Finally, if you're anti-test (like me), you can go back and do the exercise from *What Makes You Joy-Full?* or you can simply start noticing in your day-to-day what lights you up and what drains you. See if you can find a pattern of activities on both the joy-full and joy-less side. That will provide a clue as to what kinds of activities to seek out or focus on over the long run, and which you probably want to outsource or avoid at all costs.

FINDING THE *MOST* JOY-FULL PATH

Clients and colleagues ask me all the time ...

How do I know I'm on the most joy-full path?

How do I know that the actions I'm taking on my path are the most joy-full ones possible?

How do I know that my strategic plan is the most joy-full way forward?

How do I know that the service I provide / product I create is the most joy-full way to express or harness my passions and talents?

As a service provider, how do I know who my most joy-full clients are to work with?

Before we can answer any of these questions about what's *most* joy-full, you need to have a sense of what brings you joy in the first place. If you haven't answered the questions in *When Do You Feel Joy-Full?* or haven't done the *Joy Audit*, start there. If in doing those, you struggled to find joy in your current business activities, this is a great opportunity to get curious about what might create joy. You might even want to make a plan to actively explore and experiment.

Let's say that for now you have a pretty good grip on what makes you joy-full. You may want to know ...

How do I know I'm choosing the *most* joy-full option?

There are likely numerous ways for you to find the answer to this question. I'll talk about three paths here.

Listen to Your Body

One of the qualities that sets joy apart from other positive emotions is how we experience it in our body. It feels like it comes from somewhere deep within and fills us up completely. So naturally, our bodies are a great barometer of what is our most joy-full option. When you imagine yourself doing an activity (like attending an event or being interviewed on a podcast), following a path (like starting a podcast of your own or writing a book), or interacting with a person (like hiring an assistant or signing a client), do you feel a Full-Body-Hell-Yes!?

If you're reading this thinking, "Erin, I have no f*cking clue what my body would tell me. And even if it did tell me, I don't really trust it," you aren't alone. It's so common for us to be disconnected from our bodies. We are taught to listen to our rational minds when we make decisions. Many of us also have faced mental and physical health challenges that have left us distrusting and disliking our bodies. As someone who dealt with eating disorders in college and gender dysmorphia until I was in my mid-thirties, at times the last thing I've wanted to do is pay attention to my body.

So if listening to your body for a Full-Body-Hell-Yes isn't an option yet, here's how you can start to reconnect to joy as an embodied experience.

(*Note: if* **connecting** *to your body has the potential to trigger trauma or any other mental health issue, please feel free to skip this exercise and move on to the next option.*)

Close your eyes and recall a time you felt wildly joy-full. You don't need to find a moment in your business — any experience will do. Where were you? What were you doing? Who else was around? Were you indoors or outdoors? What was the temperature like? Try to recall as many details as possible, even the small ones. Now notice how your body feels as you recall. What sensations do you feel? Where do you feel them? What else can you notice about how joy shows up in your body? Really anchor into that feeling. It can now serve as a litmus test going forward. If, when you imagine, doing an activity or choosing to go down a path, your body feels similar to that moment, you've likely landed on quite a joy-full one!

If you do this activity and you don't get much of a connection with your body, that's okay. Just like you can build curiosity, creativity, and courage like a muscle, you can do the same with your connection to your body. (See the list at the end of this conversation for a variety of options.) With intentional focus on body connection, you might be surprised at how many decisions you make in your business from a place of, "Oh yeah, my body is lit up. That's a *Hell Yes!*" or just as importantly, "Nope, body's not feeling it. That's a *Hell No.*"

Is it a 10?

If you're a numbers nerd — or find listening to your body out of reach — you may love the idea of quantifying your joy. (This is a part of the book where I make a shameless plug for someone else's book ... well, books. My friend, Mark Silverman, wrote two great books called *Only 10s* and *Only 10s 2.0*[13], from which I've borrowed this concept.) The idea is simple: for any clients, projects, activities, or business strategies that you are currently engaged in or are considering taking on, ask yourself if it feels like a 10 out of 10 on the joy-full scale for you. You may know something is a 10 based on direct experience. Such as, *I am giddy every time I sit down to write a newsletter, so that's a 10 I'm going to keep doing.* Or, *I've loved working with this client in the past, so I'll absolutely work with them again.* You may also sense that something will be a 10 based on what you know about yourself, like, *It energizes me to be on stage, so exploring speaking opportunities feels like a 10.* Or, *I adore Laurie, so creating an "Amateur Hour" group experience with her sounds positively joy-full.*

Asking, "Is it a 10?" requires you to get honest with yourself and others. (That's my favorite part of this whole concept! ☺) It means saying no to things that are a 7, 8, 9, or even a 9.9! They might feel pretty joy-full, but maybe not the *most* joy-full. It often means paring down what you're doing to focus on just a few things at a time. That can be uncomfortable if you're an ambitious person who tends to have a lot on your plate. When something isn't a 10, you might have to disappoint clients, collaborators, or friends. That can also be uncomfortable if you are someone with people-pleasing tendencies. As you seek joy-full 10s, you'll need to have faith that the more you say no to non-10s, the more space you'll have for true 10s to come into your purview.

Are neither of these concepts (tuning into your body or quantifying joy) your jam? How can you get **curious** and **creative** about what is? My book coach, Patti, shared while we were writing this that for her it's all about colors. If something comes up turquoise in her mind's eye, it's a go, but if it's purple, it's a hell no. What works for *you*?

Experiment with Joy

When listening to your body isn't an option and you don't have quite enough information to be certain something is a 10, you can explore and experiment instead.

Experimentation is one of the most trusty tools in my entrepreneur tool belt. It motivates the scientist in me because it's the best way, in my opinion, to find answers you can't "think" your way into. We'll talk more in-depth about the power of experimentation and putting on your proverbial lab coat in your business later. (Curious? Start with *It's All Research* and read the four conversations that follow.) For now, just know that you can experiment with your joy in the same way you can experiment with concrete elements of your business (like marketing messages, advertising, or services/products you provide).

Wondering if creating a podcast is the most joy-full way to build an audience? Commit to a six-month trial to feel it out. Or maybe you're wondering the same about LinkedIn. And because six months is a really long time in social media terms, perhaps instead you commit to posting every day for 100 days.

Sometimes you'll need to commit to a long period of time to truly be able to assess. When I started my *Life in the And* podcast back in 2020, it took me at least three months to realize that though it was *a* joy-full path, it was not the *most* joy-full path in the context of my business at the time.

But you might reach clarity quickly. If it's joy-full AF — perhaps a 10! — keep going as long as it keeps being so. However, if it's not joy-full, you don't have to continue for the whole time period you initially committed to. My TikTok experiment worked that way for me. At one point, a mentor suggested that my personality and wisdom were perfect for TikTok. My body didn't give me much information on whether that was the most joy-full audience-building activity I could be doing, so I committed to a 100-day experiment. About two weeks into the 100 days, I was clear: TikTok might be a smart business strategy, but it wasn't a joy-full one for me.

Let's finish here by circling back to the original question: How do I know what the *most* joy-full path is? You can check in with your body, ask if it is a 10, or design an experiment, and still wonder, "Is this the *most* joy-full? Are there 11s out there that I'm missing?" The truth is, you'll likely never be able to answer that question. There are so many options for how you can build and run your business that you won't be able to test and rank them all. The goal here is not optimization — though of course, we like to optimize things! And in fact, if you're constantly questioning whether something better is out there, you're likely not allowing yourself to feel the joy of what you're doing right now. Try to let it be enough that you've found a Full-Body-Hell-Yes, a 10, or simply that you're working towards that feeling. After all, if we have endless capacity for joy, we don't have to worry so much about finding the *best* thing — we can just keep adding to our tank.

Ideas For Connecting With Your Body

(A note of caution: please check in with your body before you do any of these. Find what feels good to you. And consider professional guidance for any activities that might be linked with trauma, mental health concerns, or simply feel too unsafe in your body to do them alone.)

- Do a body scan meditation, focusing on all sensations big and small
- Practice yoga or stretch
- Do progressive muscle relaxation, tightening then releasing muscles from your head to toe
- Dance
- Deliberately engage your senses — stop and smell the roses, focus on what your food tastes like, feel your feet in the grass
- Exercise
- Spend time in nature
- Practice breath work
- Get a massage (or give one to yourself)
- Keep a journal of thoughts, emotions, and body sensations
- Create physical connection (hugs, cuddles) with loved ones and pets

CREATE METRICS FOR ~~SUCCESS~~ JOY

How do you measure success? Depending on your business, you could have any or all of these on your radar:

- Revenue
- Profit
- # of clients, customers, users, or subscribers
- Customer retention rate
- Email open rate
- # of email subscribers
- # of followers on LinkedIn, TikTok, Instagram, or Facebook
- Average # of likes, comments, shares, and saves on your social posts
- Average # of podcast listens
- # of books sold
- Conversion rate
- Quantity of referrals
- Quality of referrals

These traditional metrics of success can be important to track. For instance, if your conversion rate is low, you might want to look at your sales process to see what can be improved. Are you reaching the right clients in your marketing and outreach? Are you providing a product or service that your ideal client needs? Are you clear about what you provide? On the flip side, if your conversion rate is high, or even outpacing what you can deliver, is it time to raise your prices? Would creating new products or services that can scale to more people help you keep up with demand? Is it time to hire a team (or more people for your existing team)?

In a sea of possible metrics, it's possible to choose poor ones. Likes, comments, shares, and saves are only the tip of the iceberg of who's paying attention on social media. Low engagement does not necessarily mean low impact of your content. A large following on social media, email, or a podcast matters very little if the people in your audience aren't right for you.

These types of metrics that don't paint a full or accurate picture are joy-sucks. They're also sneaky because they are easy for our brains to get attached to. We latch onto likes and comments on our content because we can't easily imagine the size of the iceberg under the surface of people lurking. (Couldn't they have the decency to soothe our anxieties with a simple 'like'!!!??? 😒) We also chase followers because we can't fathom why more isn't always better. (If it's not, why are people still in my DMs trying to sell me followers? And why do podcasts, speaking events, and book agents look at or ask for my follower counts to decide whether my pitch is worth considering?)

There are also metrics that are poor in a more inconspicuous way. These metrics get in the way of what's important to us. They may make logical sense on the surface. Or they might be great metrics for *other* people to track. They might even be great metrics for ourselves at different points in time. At several points while writing this book, if I had used revenue or a full client roster as metrics for success, I would have been miserable. (In fact, I did make myself miserable once or twice. Some metrics for success are hard for me to untangle from my sense of self-worth even when I logically know that they mean nothing about me and that I need to prioritize other things!)

Take a moment to do a brief check-in with yourself on this. Are the things you're tracking giving you valuable information or are they joy-stealing distractions? Are they aligned with what's most important to you? What metrics do you want to keep and which do you need to get rid of or transform?

CREATE METRICS FOR ~~SUCCESS~~ JOY

Beyond the traditional metrics, there are also metrics that you won't find in books, or downloadable pdfs on the internet. You likely won't hear about them from mentors and colleagues either. That's because they are individually suited to you. Chances are, these "personal metrics for success" are also your metrics for joy.

That was certainly true for my client, Kaya. She came to a coaching session feeling like a failure. Though she'd already been an entrepreneur and coach for years, she'd told herself a story that she wasn't successful because she didn't have a college degree and she wasn't yet at the revenue level or client load of some of her colleagues. It was immediately clear to me that based on her life history and the trajectory of her business, these were not the best markers for her. So I decided to do an exercise with Kaya to help create her own measures for success.

We first brainstormed a list of what would make her feel successful. Not surprisingly, her list of feel-good metrics were wildly different from the commonly relied-upon ones:

- I say yes to the things that matter
- I am in powerful service
- My work energizes me/lights me up
- I have and am part of epic support networks

- Life is deeply meaningful
- I am building my dream home
- I create what intuition and desire call for
- I am choosing life
- I am there for my children

To give her a way to track them over time, for each one I asked her, "On a scale of one to 10 where 10 is ideal, where do you feel you are on this measure right now?" Once she had her collective numbers in front of her, we chose two for her to focus on. We made a plan for how Kaya could move the needle on each of those by just one point.

This exercise was so powerful she decided to put her new list of metrics on a giant piece of paper so she could see it on her wall. For each measure, she drew a circle with 10 pie pieces. She then colored in the number of pieces that represented her starting place. As she started moving up in each of the measures, she could color in a new piece of the pie.

For Kaya, it didn't feel right to completely banish her previous measures of revenue and client load. So we made them secondary. She knew that being in powerful service, focusing on meaningful work that energizes her, and taking time for her children would naturally lead to more impact, and therefore more revenue and higher demand for her services.

What she had just made primary — though neither of us had the word in our vocabulary at the time — was her joy.

What metrics are stealing your joy? Do you *need* to track them? If so, could they be secondary to your metrics for joy?

What metrics for joy would you like to be tracking? You can use the same exercise that Kaya did to come up with hers.

CREATE METRICS FOR ~~SUCCESS~~ JOY

MY METRICS FOR JOY

Make a list of what would (or already does) make you feel successful.

Go through each metric and assess where you are right now on a scale of 1-10, where 10 is ideal.

Then choose one or two to focus on for the next few weeks or months.

Make a specific plan on how you can move your number just one notch up towards 10.

WANT MORE JOY? FEEL YOUR PAIN

In her famous TED talk on the power of vulnerability, Brené Brown said, "When we numb our pain, we numb our joy."[14]

She said this without a particular context in mind — I'm sure she believes it's true in ALL contexts. I agree, AND I think it's imperative that we put it in the context of entrepreneurship and business.

Your business needs your full humanity. Yes, conventional business wisdom tells us to take our humanity **out** of the business as much as possible:

"Work on your business, not in it!"

"Your business isn't personal."

And certainly, success requires us to keep our emotions at bay and focus on logic and rational decision-making:

"Show up as an experimenter and a scientist. Treat everything you do like data."

"Follow tried and true strategies and formulas, not your feelings."

I'll be the first to tell you some of this conventional wisdom has its place. We'll talk more about that later in *Data Hath No Meaning* and *Put on Your Lab Coat AND Feel Your Feelings Too*. But also, bringing a scientist's mind to your business does not require you to deny your feelings. It does not mean being a robot.

And because you are reading this book, it's safe to assume that you are not here to become a robot 🤖.

Your business needs you to bring your full humanity to the table.

WANT MORE JOY? FEEL YOUR PAIN

To truly create and cultivate a joy-full AF business, you need to be willing to sit with, hold space for, and fully experience all your emotions. Not just in your personal life, but also in your business.

Your sadness.

Anger.

Depression.

Anxiety.

Frustration.

Regret.

Hurt.

Fear.

Joy without those feelings isn't joy. It's emotional bypassing / toxic positivity. Now, let me be clear. I'm not saying that you have to seek out negative emotions just so you can experience joy. I'm also not saying that if you experience negative emotions in your business that you need to keep yourself feeling them in order to experience joy elsewhere or at some other time.

What I am saying is that in the pursuit of joy, we need to be careful to not demonize, or stuff down other emotions. Be careful not to criticize or lash yourself when you inevitably feel emotions that aren't joy.

Feeling joy-full 100% of the time is not the goal. It's not even humanly possible. But you can expand your capacity for joy in your business (and your life) by expanding your capacity for all emotions.

Also, if you're thinking, "Well, what if I let myself feel all the feelings in my personal life so I can keep my business *all* joy *all* the time," I hate to break it to you: We just can't compartmentalize our emotional life like that.

You will be joy-full AF in your business when you allow that all emotions are valid and necessary, and part of our human experience.

THERE IS NO JOY WITHOUT REST

When you're tired, and stressed out ...
    When you're burned to a crisp ...
    When your mind and body just can't ...
There is no space for joy.

We cannot talk about joy without talking about rest.

If you're like me, rest feels awful. It's frustrating, depressing, and anxiety-producing. It can feel more miserable than the miserable we feel being on-the-go.

We've been programmed to avoid rest. Our toxic capitalist and white supremacist culture is about productivity and achievement. As if that's not enough to keep us in motion all the time, the business world reinforces it. The masculine, bro-y messaging that dominates business is about hustle and grind ...

Get up at 4 a.m., so you can get in a workout, respond to emails, meditate, and write your book all by 6 a.m.!

If you're not working 14-hour days, you clearly don't want success. If you're not optimizing every minute of your day, you're sabotaging yourself.

If you could be doing more and you aren't, you're lazy.

My stomach is churning as I write this. We idealize so many unhealthy behaviors.

Even if we logically understand that rest is important — and that hustle and grind culture is damaging and toxic— we still avoid it. That's because, as I said above, rest can feel like shit. And taking the amount of rest that would *truly* recharge us feels like full-on *poopy shit* (to quote one of my favorite TV characters, Alice Pieszecki from *The L World*).

That's because our nervous systems react to us slowing down. For one, we are actively rebelling against internalized capitalism, patriarchy, and white supremacy. These systems of oppression fuel our hustle-and-grind culture, our over-focus on achievement, and our belief that work and output determine our value as people. We absorb the messages generated by these systems daily; sometimes in overt ways, but most of the time, more subtly. We've also been absorbing these messages since birth, and as a result, they have become embedded in our nervous systems. We're not even cognitively aware of how they impact us. So when we start to act out against them, our nervous systems flare up, as if we are doing something wrong.

On top of our nervous systems reacting to internalized oppression, they are also responding to physiological changes that happen when we slow down. When we go, go, go, we run on adrenaline and cortisol. Sometimes we ride on these hormones for years. The minute we begin to slow down, those hormones stop firing as much, and our bodies feel their withdrawal.

As if that's not enough for our systems to bear, we also start to feel things, emotionally and physically, that we've been ignoring. Society rewards intellectualism and living in our heads — so we actively stuff down emotions and ignore physical sensations. But if we slow down and rest, the emotions come bubbling to the top and so does the pain and exhaustion that our bodies have been holding at bay as we grit our teeth, grinding our way through what we've been schooled to believe is the way to success.

Instead of rest being a relief and a recharge, all these sensations added up feel like a bad hangover. Or as Simone Seol says in an Instagram post, "Rest [...] is ACTIVE DETOX. Detox feels bad. Very bad. If detox felt pleasant, no one would ever struggle with addiction." EXACTLY, Simone! Who in their right mind would voluntarily go through that? It makes so much sense why we'd avoid that discomfort by continuing to hustle and grind, or by telling ourselves we're resting while still answering emails or diving into work-related books on the beach, or even why we'd cut our rest short.

But the more that we don't allow ourselves to truly rest, and the more we neglect our feelings, bodies, and nervous systems — the further away we get from joy.

We *have* to rest. We need courage to let go of the lies we've been told about our worth and laziness, to feel the feelings we've been stuffing down for so long, and to listen to what our body's aches and pains are telling us. It requires immense self-compassion to face whatever comes up. When you have courage, self-compassion, and the willingness to meet what arises in the resting process, you will make space for joy. And in making space for joy, you will welcome the whole of your humanity — thoughts, feelings, and nervous system. Your whole humanity is worth resting for.

Imagine what might be possible for our society if we all allowed ourselves more rest.

WHAT IS THIS, AMATEUR HOUR? (THE JOY OF BEING A NEWBIE)

Yes, yes it is!

Call it what you will. Beginner. Newbie. Amateur.

I once thought these were insulting terms. When you're new to something, the assumption is that you're not that good at it. You might even be downright *bad* at it. I used to hate being bad at things. I especially hated being bad at things in front of other people. More so if that particular thing was really important to me.

When I first started coaching, I loathed the thought of someone experiencing or witnessing my coaching and concluding that I was bad at it. I was afraid of the judgments people would make about my competence, capabilities, and worthiness. At least that's what I told myself. In truth, I was more afraid that their assessments were true. (I've since learned that the only time other people's judgments affect us are when we believe there is a kernel of truth to them.) Thoughts like, "Who does Erin think they are? What a shitty coach!" and "They are foolish to think they can make it as a coach!" were what I imagined others saying, but really I was thinking them myself. The more I saw the gap between where I was skill-wise as a coach and where I wanted to be, the more my Inner Critic lashed me.

The only solution I saw was to try to be masterful and perfect as quickly as possible. I motivated myself using fear and shame, rather than using a growth mindset of curiosity, courage, and celebration of progress. Being a beginner, for me, completely sucked the joy out of learning and growing as a coach.

I know I'm not alone in having a joy-sucking relationship with being new or inexperienced at something. My clients bring this to me all the time. They are worried that if other people see them being weak at some skill, people will see them as stupid, incompetent, foolish, or silly. Of course, since judgment only matters if you believe there's truth to it, my clients are actually worried that they will see themselves as stupid, incompetent, foolish, and silly. Some clients also worry that people will spread rumors or gossip about them, which will, in their minds, inevitably lead to business failure. So, like me, they internally criticize themselves for not yet being at the level of mastery they expect of themselves. In some cases, clients have considered not starting a new endeavor at all — it's felt safer than experiencing the judgment they believe is inevitable. Others have decided to give being a beginner a whirl but have given up when they aren't immediately brilliant at their new skill.

Another reason we resist being new at something is that it's a lot of work. We have to put in more effort at the outset than when we've mastered it. Imagine learning to drive a car. At first, you have to think about each step:

"Okay, I have to push the pedal (A little more? What, maybe less?) and then I have to put two hands on the steering wheel (Crap, where do they go when I turn?!) and then eyes on the road (Where am I supposed to focus again? Am I seeing all the signs?), and wait, hold on — let me go back and check my rear-view mirrors (Can I see everything I'm supposed to?). Oh God, what am I forgetting!?"

Of course, as time goes on, all of that becomes automatic, and your focus is less on *how* you are driving and more on *where* you are heading.

When we start something new, we may convince ourselves we are starting off with a blank slate. So, we conclude in advance that we're going to be bad at it for some amount of time and it will demand an awful lot of effort to get good. No wonder we lose our joy! In reality, especially in business, we rarely come into something with absolutely no transferable experience or skills. Chances are, we are vastly underestimating ourselves.

I mentioned earlier that when I started coaching, I hated the idea of people judging my coaching. One of the reasons I hated it so much was that I assumed that I was at a much lower competency than I was. I hadn't considered that over the last decade, I'd built up a ton of skills that gave me the foundation of a good coach already. I wasn't as much of a beginner as I thought.

As a user experience researcher at Facebook and Microsoft, my job was to listen deeply to people, to hear not just what they were saying, but to consider what was going on for them underneath. If a research participant asked, "Can we move this button from here to here?" my job was to uncover what was behind that question. What need or want would moving that button fulfill for them? And could we even fulfill it in other (and better) ways? As a coach, I'm always looking for what's bubbling beneath the surface. That's where sustainable, long-term transformation happens. Another part of my job as a researcher was to pull together data points — from things people said in interviews or responses to surveys — and draw out connections and insights. I'm constantly doing the same thing with clients, except rather than gathering data across multiple people, I'm gathering data about a single person across time. I often notice things about people that they'd never considered until I highlight the patterns I see.

In my leadership roles at both companies, I helped people learn and grow as researchers and people. Part of that was helping them discover their superpowers. Another part was helping them understand their inner voices, especially the ones that were in the way of the impact they wanted to make or the goals they wanted to achieve. What I didn't realize until I started coaching-specific training was that I was just as much a coach as I was a manager. I just hadn't been called a coach.

Even if you are starting something that feels completely new to you, I want to invite you to dig a little deeper for where that might not be true. I tried visual art for a few months, explicitly to learn to cultivate joy in being bad at something. I couldn't imagine that I had any skills whatsoever, but I realized that I did have some art knowledge from growing up with parents who collected, and I had a decent understanding of color theory from working with visual designers in the tech world. (That being said, I was just as bad at art as I thought I was. Sometimes you won't be the blank slate you think you are and sometimes you'll find out that you're actually bad at something. Art for me as an exercise in learning to be okay with being bad at something, and realizing that being bad didn't mean diddly squat about me.)

So, sometimes you'll be less of a beginner than you think. And sometimes you'll actually be a beginner. When I was adamant that "beginner" was a dirty word, I didn't realize that there are plenty of upsides to being new at something. Those upsides are a great source of joy.

We'll dive into those upsides in a moment, but before we do, it's helpful to start by looking at the myths and downsides of being a master or expert. Here are some common beliefs we hold about masters:

- Mastery is a goal we should aspire to achieve.
- Once we have mastered something, it becomes easy.
- Masters don't fail as often as non-masters.
- People don't judge masters.
- Masters don't worry about judgment or other people's feedback.
- Masters have quiet or non-existent inner critics. They are confident in their capabilities and their worth.

Those beliefs all have some kernel of truth to them. But they're not completely true. Here are some things that can *also* be true about masters:

- Masters can have unreasonably high expectations of themselves. They put a lot of pressure on themselves to meet those expectations.
- Masters can believe they aren't supposed to fail. So they don't give themselves a lot of permission to — and they can beat themselves up when they do.

- Masters, in efforts not to fail, can sometimes take fewer risks than beginners.
- Masters can believe that others have high expectations for them, too. The fear of judgment doesn't magically go away as they become more masterful. In some ways, it can intensify. Being seen as bad at something as a master can feel way worse than as a beginner who is "supposed to be bad"!
- Masters can get stuck in rules, boxes, and how it's always been done before. They can even get stuck in a notion of what constitutes mastery (such as, master coaches do X, Y, and Z).

As I read these, many of them resonate for me. As I've become more masterful as a coach, at times, I've trapped myself in my own expectations, given myself less permission to take risks with my clients, and stayed more within a box of what I think good coaching is. Not only is none of that a recipe for joy, it's also not a recipe for powerfully serving my clients! When I notice myself falling into these traps, I know it's time to come back to a beginner's mind.

Let's come back to that, too. The downsides of mastery are precisely the upsides of being a beginner:

- Beginners have permission to screw up. In fact, it's more likely that people expect them to make mistakes than to be perfect. It comes with the territory of learning a new skill. (So already, being a beginner comes with a lot less pressure than you might have initially thought.)
- Beginners have much more freedom to take risks, because they have much more permission for those risks to not pan out.
- Beginners don't always have the knowledge or know-how that masters do. They don't know the rules, or the boxes they're supposed to fit in, or even what it means to be "masterful." Which means, beginners tend to break the rules. At times, beginners are more innovative than masters!

Beginners have a greater ability and more permission to tap into their curiosity, creativity, and courage than masters.

Early on in my coaching, I learned techniques that felt weird to me. They involved having people check in with where they felt thoughts and beliefs lived in their bodies. These techniques dealt with emotions on a much deeper level than I imagined I'd be going into as a coach. I wasn't quite convinced that they were as impactful as my teachers made them out to be. Most of my coaching clients at the time were people I'd known previously — colleagues from Facebook and Microsoft, and friends from other points in my life. They knew I was a beginner. They also trusted me. They were always game for me trying on some of these "weird" techniques with them. I still feel that those early sessions were some of my best. I took the pressure off of myself for what I was doing to "work" and got curious about what might happen.

With all this upside of being a beginner, am I saying that we should never become masters? Absolutely not. It's not possible if you continue to sharpen your knowledge and skills. Instead, I believe the recipe for joy is two-fold: finding joy in being a beginner when you actually are AND finding ways to keep a *beginner's mind* as you move toward mastery. What if masters had just as much allowance to screw up, take risks, and break rules!? We'd have to re-write the definition of a "master!"

If you're not convinced that being a beginner or keeping a beginner's mind can be a source of joy, take some comfort in knowing that neuroplasticity research supports this. Our brains are quite malleable throughout the course of our lifetimes. They will make new neuronal connections all the time. One of the best ways to create new connections is through learning. Dr. David Eagleman, a professor at Stanford and CEO of Neosensory, wrote *Livewired: The Inside Story of the Ever-Changing Brain*[15] and spoke about it on

Brené Brown's *Unlocking Us* podcast[16]. He shared that not only do our brains benefit from learning new things, they also benefit from us being *bad* at them. Say what!!?? Here I was hating being bad at new things, and I was taking care of my brain health! Eagleman also said that we need to put in the effort that we so dread to become good at things so that we can create and rewire neural pathways. It's not enough to simply be bad. We have to be bad for a while and keep up the effort to become better in order to maximize the benefits to our brains.

So perhaps you can now join me in the joy of being bad at something. If you're looking for ideas, make a list of, "It would be joy-full for me to be bad at ____," and tackle them one by one. I never became a visual artist, but I did enjoy the couple months that I made bad art. And perhaps along with the joy of being bad, you can also join me in the joy of having a beginner's mind no matter how good you are at the things you do!

YOU CAN'T IMAGINE YET WHAT'S OVER THE HORIZON
(THE JOY OF PLAYING "THE LONG GAME")

> *"There was always a large horizon. There is much to be done … It's up to you to contribute some small part to a program of human betterment for all time."*
>
> ~ Francis Perkins

Chances are, you haven't heard of Francis Perkins. It's even less likely you know her if you don't live in the United States. Even if you do, Perkins isn't a prominent figure in American history, despite contributing so much to our current reality. She was the Secretary of Labor in Franklin Delano Roosevelt's (FDR) cabinet in the 1930s and was the driving force behind the creation of some of America's basic social safety nets and labor laws, including social security, unemployment insurance, aid to the homeless, maternal and child welfare, the 40-Hour Workweek, minimum wage, and banning child labor.

Let me say this: I'm not writing about Francis Perkins in a book on joy in business for political reasons. Although her story is inspiring from a political perspective, I'm writing about her because of how she became the driving force behind so many monumental changes and what we can learn about joy from her story.

In 1911, twenty years before joining FDR's administration, she was visiting a friend in New York City when they heard sirens and came outside to see a clothing factory on fire. It was an event called the Triangle Shirtwaist Fire and it killed 147 people. She knew immediately that she wanted to get involved in a mission to end factory fires. Gradually, over many years, she became an influential figure in policy work within New York's city and state governments. To her surprise, as time went on, her mission and goals expanded.

YOU CAN'T IMAGINE YET WHAT'S OVER THE HORIZON

By the time she was invited to serve as Secretary of Labor for the FDR administration, factory fires were just one small piece of a larger effort to protect workers and promote employment during the Great Depression.

When I read Perkins' story in a newsletter a few years ago, I took away two powerful messages that are relevant to joy-full AF business. One takeaway comes from the quote at the top of this conversation: "There's always a large horizon." She was committed to her mission for the long haul. Her biggest contribution didn't come until 20 years into her work. Had she been narrowly focused on the short term, she might have given up. Or she might have even seen her work as complete once city and state legislatures created better policies around factories. Who knows what the US would have looked like for the last 90 years had she not played a longer game.

Remembering that business is a long game is a challenge. We tend to plan and evaluate our progress in annual, quarterly, or even monthly chunks. We set annual revenue targets. We pay quarterly taxes. We look at month-over-month audience growth. When we overly zoom in on the short-term decisions and metrics, we can lose sight of the fact that we're really aiming to be in business over the long haul, whether that's for a few years or a few decades. We also lose sight of how our here-and-now decisions contribute (or not) to that future. If we find ourselves not meeting short-term goals, we may feel miserable, or even want to throw in the towel, forgetting that some of our biggest impact and achievements might be still years ahead of us.

The other powerful takeaway from Perkins' story is that she could not have predicted where the long game would take her. She initially set out to fix a disastrous problem she saw in the present — factory fires. She had no way to predict in 1911 that following her passion would expand into a bigger mission, or that she would eventually become part of a presidential cabinet. I suspect that Francis Perkins knew something that many of us don't: the map you have of what's possible right now is based on what you know to be true ... *right now*. It represents all the knowledge and experience you have gathered from past experience and other people. But the future does not stay within the boundaries of the past. Otherwise, our lives would be very predictable and boring. Everything you do in your business has the potential to open new opportunities to explore — and to expand you into uncharted territory on the map. We'll talk in *Fe-Fi-Fo-Fum ... Plant Some Magic Beans* about ways you can keep your eyes on expanding that territory through intentionally planting seeds...err, Magic Beans ... of joy that may sprout into new opportunities and directions in the future.

Shortly before I started my business, I had a conversation with my financial advisor, who is also a dear family friend. She was fully in support of me starting a business under one condition: "Erin, you have to promise me that you'll stay in business for at least five years." When the COVID-19 pandemic hit, she told me to add another year on to that promise. And then as the pandemic dragged on, she continued to ask me to add more years. What JoAnna knows better than anyone is that it takes time to build a business and that the world operates in cycles. "You can't know until at least five years in whether you have a profitable or viable business. There are too many factors that contribute to success or lack thereof, including world politics and economics, to make sense of data on any shorter time scale."

We may not achieve our goals in the first six months, year, or two years that we're in business. No matter what business you are in, it takes time to develop things like your brand and customer base. It may also take time to master your craft. I know I become an exponentially better coach every year. My clients who are speakers, writers, and social media content creators tell me that the quality of their thoughts and the potency of their wisdom came from keeping at it for a really long time.

What's possible for your joy knowing that no matter where you are right now, there is much more to come and that you can't even imagine from where you are standing what it might look like? What might you do differently in the short-term (what activities would you do, or goals would you set) if your focus was also on the large horizon?

FE-FI-FO-FUM ...
PLANT SOME MAGIC BEANS

> *"Stop my boy! I'll swap your cow for magic beans. They'll bring you lots of joy."*
>
> - Jack and the Beanstalk

I have a quart-sized jar of jellybeans on my desk. These are my Magic Beans. Every time I "plant" a Magic Bean in my business, a jellybean goes into the jar.

As we talked about in *Focus on the Present ... But Not Too Much*, being overly focused on the present, and on what results we're creating *right now* can cost us joy. We limit ourselves by only doing activities that we believe will have immediate payoff. It's understandable that we fall into this trap. Because we can't predict the future, instant payoffs produce a sense of security. They can also give us validation that our efforts are not being wasted, or an indication that we're on the right path.

Businesses, like gardens, take time to grow. Not every planted seed will sprout. And of those that do, most won't sprout right away. If you planted a garden based on what would sprout quickly, you'd miss out on a whole variety of vegetables and plants.

If you've heard the idea of "planting seeds" before, it's probably because it's a popular one in business and personal development. Personally, I find that language and metaphor limiting. Which is why my seeds are Magic Beans. By the end of this conversation, I hope you will see yours that way too and be excited by the joy-fullness they can create in your business!

Unlike sowing a garden, you don't always know when you're planting a Magic Bean. In 2016, a Magic Bean proverbially fell out of my pocket when I flew to a weekend conference in New York City put on by Ramit Sethi called Forefront. The event was largely geared toward entrepreneurs, and though I was on the management path at Facebook at the time, something nudged me to go. I had no idea when I lingered a little longer than planned at a post-conference dinner that one of the people who joined us late, Caitlin Padgett, would become my first coach nearly a year later. Or that she'd introduce me to some of my closest friends, help me make life-changing decisions around my gender identity, and be the catalyst for me leaving corporate and becoming a coach myself. All I knew getting on the plane to the event was that flying across the country to hang out with 500 strangers was a growth edge for me, and I hoped it would bring me a few days of joy.

And unlike vegetables and flowers, when we plant a Magic Bean, it's not clear what could sprout. It's not like putting a zucchini seed in the ground and then, lo and behold, a zucchini pops up a little later. A virtual coffee date might sprout into a new client, collaborator, a referral months or years down the road. That doesn't mean all Beans are ambiguous. If we speak at a conference, we may sense that at least one new client could come our way. But I've found that more often than not, what sprouts is not necessarily what we expected.

Along with not always knowing *what* will sprout, we also can't predict *when* they will sprout. A zucchini takes six to eight weeks. A Magic Bean? Who knows! It could be immediate. But it could just as easily germinate months or years from now.

In early 2020, I attended a conference in Washington, D.C. Though a part of me secretly hoped I'd walk away from the conference with new clients, another part of me knew to go in with no agenda. This was a community I was unfamiliar with and a bit intimidated by. I had no idea if they were "my people" or if the topics on the conference agenda would light me up. At the end of the conference, I knew I had planted a Magic Bean or two, but I wasn't sure if any would sprout, or if they did, what they'd turn into. About a week later, one of the Beans sprouted when someone I had spent time with at the conference reached out about working with me. Another sprouted six months later (which in the early COVID-19 days felt like years) when a coach I'd spent quite a bit of time getting to know at the conference referred me to the daughter of one of his clients. She was an ideal fit and became one of my longest-term clients. If I'd been too wrapped up in finding new clients at the conference, I would have missed out on the joy of getting to know the coach, and he likely would have not referred me. I wouldn't be surprised at this point if there are still more Magic Beans yet to sprout from that conference!

I have a story that illustrates how long a Magic Bean can wait to sprout. In 2015, I was interviewed by the American Psychological Association about my non-traditional career path. In 2022, Stony Brook University's psychology department invited me to speak to their graduate students about non-traditional career paths. When I asked how they found me, it was that 2015 article — seven years that Bean was waiting to sprout! Thankfully, Stony Brook was open to me talking about any part of my path, so I spoke about coaching and entrepreneurship instead of Facebook. And who knows, if or what that Stony Brook speaking opportunity might sprout into later.

So, like me with Forefront in 2016, we don't always know that we're planting a Bean. And again, even when we do know, we don't always know if it will sprout. We also mostly don't know what it will sprout into or when. That, my friend, is not a run-of-the-mill garden; it's magic!

Imagine what might be possible in your garden (or the forests of your business wilderness, if that metaphor suits you better), if you pursued joy-full activities in the here and now, and then got curious about what might end up growing in the future as a result. It's a double dip of joy! You get it now planting it and again whenever that Bean magically sprouts in the future.

Magic Beans are one of my favorite ways to regularly create and cultivate joy. They not only fill a jar full of colorful jellybeans, they also help me keep my joy tank full. If you're not sure what counts as a Magic Bean, I want to reassure you that almost anything can.

The only "rule" is that you don't go in with an agenda about what, how, or when a Bean might sprout. That practically guarantees it to lose its magical properties. Here are a few ideas to get you started:

- Virtual coffee dates with old friends and colleagues
- Writing email newsletters
- Attending conferences, events or workshops on topics that interest you
- Going to networking events
- Giving talks or workshops
- Attending local meetups
- Putting out a podcast
- Guesting on a podcast
- Posting on social media
- Engaging with people on social media through DMs and comments

You may notice that all these ideas are business-relevant. But here's a sneaky secret — *some of the most magical of Beans come when you aren't even trying to plant them.* They'll come when you aren't necessarily thinking about your business. You can and *will* plant Magic Beans purely by pursuing joy in all areas of your life. I've met several clients at social meetups, parties, and through friends of friends. Some of my clients have met clients and collaborators on airplanes, golf courses, and tennis courts. You can plant a Magic Bean in any activity you do — you never know when you'll meet somebody who will open a door or show you a path that you hadn't yet seen.

I keep my joy tank full by planting one Magic Bean (or more) every day. As I watch my jellybean jar fill, I know that even when

I'm going through challenges or droughts in the business, things are always bubbling away beneath the surface.

MAGIC BEAN BRAINSTORM

Make a list of at least 100 activities you could do to plant a Magic Bean. Don't limit yourself to activities that you believe will create sprouts. Remember, any activity could turn into something magical in the future. Once you have a list, make a daily or weekly planting plan. And notice if your planting plan starts to suck away your joy. The magic is in following your joy, not a strict schedule.

If you like having something to look at, find a jar and fill it with anything that feels joy-full. I, for one, love the colorfulness of Jelly Belly beans, but I know many folks would not be able to keep themselves from eating them. Thankfully, my sweet tooth craves other things!

PUT ON YOUR HILA HAT

We've covered several traps that we can fall into when setting goals (*Heading Toward Destinations on Other People's Maps, Going After Possible Goals, Chasing Happiness, Chasing Enoughness*). It's not just what goals we set, though, that can either cultivate or drain our joy — it's also about how we chase them.

Recall that we sometimes infer that achieving our goals says something about us — that we're competent, capable, and/or worthy (Trap #4). We also make failure mean something too — that we are none of those things. So if *success* = *worthy* and *failure* = *not worthy*, then reaching our goals becomes a high-stakes, all-or-nothing endeavor. We then become needy, anxious, or clenching in our energy. We take fewer risks and put blinders on, focusing only on activities that move us toward the goal, rather than seeing opportunities along the path to try out new ideas or pivot completely.

> The more we tie our self-worth or happiness to accomplishing the goal, the more hell-bent we get on reaching it at all costs.

If we want to get out of the meaning-making trap, we can change which goals we go after. But that may not always be a solution. It's not necessarily the goal itself that is the problem. It's our attachment to reaching it. Often a better option is to change *how* we go after our goals. One of the most joy-full ways to change your "how" is to use HILA: high intention toward reaching the goal and low attachment to if, when, or how you get there. Back in the Introduction I mentioned that when I visualized HILA I saw it as a hat to wear while adventuring towards different destinations in the business wilderness.

Let's unpack HILA a bit, because it can be easily misunderstood. Being highly intentional means putting plans in place and taking steps toward reaching the goal. We'd LOVE to get there. But, having low attachment means that along the way we are open to shifts. Maybe we'll need to be creative about the steps we are taking toward the goal. We might need to take a right turn here, or a left turn there. Maybe we'll need to take longer to reach our goal than we originally hoped. Or maybe the goal itself will need to change. When we're open to shifts, we might even discover a better goal to go after.

Being in HILA also allows us to tap into three of the foundational ingredients of joy: curiosity, creativity, and courage.

Curiosity. We can ask ourselves questions like: I wonder how I can get to my goal? I wonder what I can do next? I wonder what's possible?

Creativity. When the path doesn't have to be set, we can lean into creative ways to get where we want to go. And when we hit inevitable roadblocks, creativity can help us change course or find a path forward.

Courage. We can take risks, stretch ourselves, do things we've never done before. And because we aren't attached to if or when we get to the finish line, we can fail, fail, fail, and fail again.

It might seem counterintuitive to set a goal that you aren't attached to achieving. It definitely felt this way for me when I first considered it. But, I've landed on a moon metaphor (pun intended) that soothes the parts of me that don't understand why I'd ever go after a goal that I'm not sure I'll reach. See, if we're too attached to reaching the moon, we may not allow ourselves to see all the opportunities for landing elsewhere. Maybe by tweaking our course, we could go even farther than planned, landing on Mars instead. Or maybe as we fly out of Earth's atmosphere, we'll hear a noise off to the left (yes, I know there's no sound in space, stick with me here!), and follow it to a wild party at the International Space Station. If we're truly unattached to if, when, or how we get to the moon, we may decide to hang out in Earth's orbit for a little while and take a little rest, before getting back on track to the moon. Or we might even decide to stay in Earth's orbit forever because that's pretty great. All of this to say that when you're overly attached to a particular destination, you miss all kinds of opportunities for joy.

Had I not put on my HILA Hat while writing a book, *Joy-Full AF* would not exist. When I first started (as I mentioned in *Why Did I Write a Book on Joy-full AF Business?*), I had a book idea about the word "And." Had I been overly attached to that idea, I would have written something that was maybe okay, but not what really lit my heart up. However, because I committed to HILA (I even publicly announced I was "HILA-ing" my book on Facebook!), when I realized the proverbial moon was no longer my destination, I gave myself permission to hang out in the Earth's orbit until I found a new direction. It took several iterations, and several more pauses along the way, to land at *Joy-Full AF*. The book in your hands is so much more powerful, and comes to you with so much more love in its words because of my willingness to stay unattached to what book I wrote.

HILA was not just about what book I wrote, though. It was also about if and when a book came out. This part of HILA was admittedly a bit more difficult for me to stick to. I was eager to get my words out in the world! But sure enough, every time I tried to set a deadline for myself, my energy clenched, I stressed, and I lost the joy. As soon as I put my HILA Hat back on around timelines, everything eased, creativity flowed, and I had more fun.

The last bit of HILA in writing this book came mid-process when I figured out that I needed to also be unattached to *how* I wrote the book. As I mentioned, the best way for me to write the first draft of this book ended up being by speaking it into Otter. AI. I also wrote it in conversations rather than traditional chapters. If I'd made my non-traditional writing process mean something about my capability or worth (or even whether or not I'm allowed to call myself a writer) it simply would not exist.

So how do you put on your HILA Hat? Take a look at the list of goals you have for your business right now. You may want to revisit the goals you listed in the exercise in *Falling Into Multiple Traps at Once*.

Are there any goals you already have naturally *high intention* and *low attachment* toward reaching? Great! You're already set up for joy in going after those.

How about goals where you have *low intention* and *low attachment toward* reaching them? You don't really want to go after them and you don't think it means anything about you if you don't reach them. I call these **Apathy Goals**. There's no joy in going after them. Throw them out completely.

Are there any goals you have *low intention* and *high attachment* to? You don't really want to go after them, but unlike Apathy Goals you think reaching those goals will mean something about you or bring you happiness. (If you're having a hard time wrapping your brain around a goal like this, I like the example of someone who doesn't want to be a manager in a corporate role, but goes after a promotion because they think it will signal they are good enough.) I call these **Should Goals**. As we've talked about in many conversations, *should* is a joy-suck! There are two options for these kinds of goals. Like Apathy Goals you can throw these out completely too. There's no sense in going after something you don't want. Or, you can ask yourself, what would turn this Should Goal into a **Want Goal** by shifting it from *low intention* to *high intention*? Once you have the want, or it's already clear what your want is, you may still have high attachment to getting there. We'll look at how to lower your attachment next.

Lastly, are there any goals (either from the original list or after changing some goals to Want Goals) where you have *high intention* and *high attachment*? You really want to get there and you believe it means something about you or your happiness if you do. Here are some questions you can ask yourself to lower your attachment:

- What's the *worst* that could happen if I don't achieve the goal?
- What's the *best* that could happen if I don't achieve the goal?

- What does it mean about me or my success if I don't achieve that goal?
- What will it mean about me or my success if I do achieve the goal?
- How can I move from clenching into curiosity? What specific steps can I take to do that?
- What do I need to let go of in order to lower my attachment?

You may notice that these questions are geared toward helping you shift away from outcomes as a metric of your success, worth, and emotional well-being. But once you have your HILA Hat on for a goal, you still may want to know, "How can I make the process even more joy-full?"

Here are some additional questions to ask yourself:

- What route would be the most fun to take towards my goal?
- What are some creative ways of getting there that I haven't thought of yet?
- What can I get curious about as I take each step?
- Where can I lean into fear, take risks, or stretch myself?

See what shifts in your business if you continuously wear your HILA Hat! If your experience is at all like mine, the twists and turns — even when frustrating — will be worth the unexpected directions you end up going!

[Before we move on, I should note that sometimes we resist putting on our HILA Hat because we're afraid of what others will think of us if we change our goal mid-progress. Unfortunately, it's true that people will judge. No matter what your reason, some people will see pivoting as flaky or uncommitted. But others will see it as inspiring and give them permission to do the same. I've found that when even one person tells me I've inspired them or given them permission to pivot or change, it immediately evaporates the weight of any judgment or criticism I may have received. You can't escape judgment no matter *what* you do. It's not only futile to try, it's a drain on your joy. If you can't please everyone, why not please yourself and follow your joy instead?]

IT'S ALL FUN AND GAMES ... NO, REALLY!

I've said throughout that joy is about much more than fun and delight. But sometimes it IS about just that! Sometimes intentionally infusing fun and delight into your work gets your creative juices going. Sometimes you move faster towards your goals ... or even go further than you originally planned. And sometimes a little fun can move you through fear, challenge, and doubt in ways you can't when just tapping into your courage.

Gamification — the process of adding games or gamelike elements to an activity — has been popular for decades (McDonald's started their famous Monopoly game back in the late 80s), and has become even more widespread in the digital age. When I worked at Facebook on the content sharing team in 2017, we studied other apps that gamified content sharing (like Snapchat's "Streaks" of snapping with a friend at least once in a 24-hour period for more than 3 days) to see what we might incorporate into the Facebook experience. (Side note: nothing we considered made it past initial ideation. I'm personally grateful that neither Facebook or Instagram went down the gamification path, despite adopting several other successful features of Snapchat.) Gamification has become so popular that even some of my games have been gamified. Words with Friends allows me to collect coins by playing a certain number of words or taking certain actions in the app, and those coins can then be traded in for word hints and free tile swaps. My New York Times Crossword app tracks how many days I've completed a crossword without hints, and tracks my average completion times. Of course, I can't help but want to do even the hardest of puzzles as fast as possible, knowing that I might be able to beat my own record!

My examples may suggest that gamification is a dark psychology tactic for keeping people addicted to their phones — or in McDonald's case buying more Big Macs, chicken nuggies, and fries. It certainly can be. But it can also be a great way to stay motivated and consistent towards a goal. When you create games in your business, you can tap into at least three of the four ingredients of joy: **curiosity, creativity,** and **courage.**

So why might you create a game? I mentioned a few at the beginning of this conversation, but I'll repeat them and add a few more here:

- To have more fun! You don't need any justification to be playful!
- To take pressure off the work that you're doing. Some people thrive in pressure, but many don't. For me, there's a sweet spot, and games can help me alleviate just enough pressure that I can feel excited about my work again.
- To shift your focus away from outcomes/results so that you can be more present in the process of achieving your goals. As we talked about in several conversations (*Goal Traps, Put on Your HILA Hat*), we can lose joy when we are overly attached to and focused on the outcome.
- To move through a fear or challenge.

To give you a sense of what I mean by playing games, here are a couple I've played in my business. You can adopt them exactly how I describe them or adapt them any way that suits your needs. (And if creating your own game is more your jam, we'll talk about how you can do just that little later in this conversation.)

Collecting Nos

No matter what business you're in, you are going to experience people saying "No" to you or what you have to offer. Most of us hate the word "No." We don't like saying it to other people and we certainly don't like hearing it. It's a rejection and sometimes our brains can't differentiate between a rejection of an offer and a rejection of *us*. Even for the most confident and self-assured people, rejection can feel painful. Painful enough that it's worth actively avoiding. The fear of rejection can be so overwhelming at times that it leaves us paralyzed.

Collecting Nos is my favorite way to move through this fear or stuckness. The rules are simple: Set a target of how many Nos you want to collect either in a specific activity (like collect 20 Nos to guesting on a podcast) or across a period of time (like collect 20 Nos in a week). You can play the game in the context of something you've been afraid of or putting off in your business — like raising your fees — or purely to work on your fear of rejection. The latter is what my friend Candace did a few years ago.

Inspired by a TED talk called, "What I Learned from 100 Days of Rejection," Candace headed to a local mall and filmed herself *Collecting Nos*. Her goal was to collect 10 Nos in 100 minutes. She asked mall goers and shop employees for ridiculous things, including to work behind the counter at a pretzel shop, to give a stranger a haircut in the mall corridor, and to purchase just one shoe from a pair. She even asked if she could take home a $20 baby shark stuffed animal for free. To her surprise, the person said, "Yes!" In fact, she got more than one yes that day. On top of realizing that you can't always predict what people might say yes to, she also learned a profound lesson about No — even when people thought her request was preposterous, nothing bad happened. She was okay. She was safe. And the more she upped the ridiculousness of the request, the more fun she had. Candace probably could have convinced herself that rejection was safe through mindset work, but nothing could have come close to what her body knew thanks to experiencing it firsthand.

Networking Bingo

Are you one of those weirdos that actually likes networking? Do you find it naturally fun, easy, or dare I say, joy-full? If so, this game isn't for you and you can move on to the next one. (And would you mind teaching the rest of us the magic of your ways?)

Okay, if you're still here, this game is my secret weapon. Though I am quite social, I was very shy for the first few decades of my life, and that still shows up at times in networking situations. It happens most often when I'm in a room of strangers and I am unsure what we might have in common.

Most people don't like networking because it's socially awkward. We don't know what to say or ask. If the other person is also having trouble keeping the flow of conversation going, it becomes doubly awkward.

Before I tell you about the game, I want to shift your perspective on networking and meeting new people in general. Often we associate networking with selling ourselves or our business to other people. What if that's a backwards approach? What if the whole point is not to figure out what to say or how to sell yourself, but instead, to figure out what you can learn about other people?

From that perspective, networking can be a fantastic place to exercise your curiosity. Being curious about other people is all about asking great questions. But, what if you don't always know what questions to ask on the spot? That's where creating *Networking Bingo* before you head to the event comes in handy!

Spend some time thinking about what would be fun to know about others or fun to experience. It could be business-related, but it doesn't have to be. Maybe you want to see if you can have an entire conversation without the other person asking you a single question. That's a Bingo Square. Maybe you want to see if you can get the person to name a weird quirk about themselves. That's a Bingo Square. Be as creative and silly as you want. Tuck your "Bingo card" away on a note card in your pocket or make a note of things on your phone to score later. Even if you don't nail all your Bingo squares, I guarantee you'll have some joy-full, interesting conversations!

The 90 Day $ Game

Collecting Nos and *Networking Bingo* are both different ways of moving through fear, challenge, and discomfort. This next game can help take the pressure off your work and/or shift your focus from outcomes/results towards joy in the process. I learned the *90 Day $ Game* from Rich Litvin. He taught it in the context of revenue goals, but any quantifiable goal could be turned into a game. And of course, the 90-day timeframe is flexible too. For example, I once helped a leader at a small start-up design a Quarter 2 User Growth game (catchy title, I know). For explaining the game, though, let's stick to what Rich Litvin originally taught me.

As we've talked about in several of the *Goal Traps*, revenue goals can be joy-sucks. We can take on revenue goals that we've seen from others because we believe that's what we should aspire to. And we can get overly attached to reaching those goals, thinking that success or failure means something about our capability and worth. One of the additional challenges of revenue as a goal is that it's a lagging indicator — that is, revenue comes in only after a series of other things have happened. For instance, in my coaching practice, how much money I've brought in is a lagging indicator of how many clients I have enrolled, and how many clients I have enrolled is a lagging indicator of how many potential clients I've had introductory coaching sessions with. And of course, how many people I've had these sessions with depends on how many people I've invited to a coaching conversation, or how many people have reached out to me through social media, my website, or referrals. All those actions leading up to revenue are leading indicators. When we attach our feelings of success and worth to a lagging indicator like revenue, we lose focus on the leading indicators. The leading indicators are our opportunity to lean into joy. They are also rife for gamification.

In the *90 Day $ Game*, you set a money goal that feels like a courageous stretch, but not impossible. As we discussed in *Goal Trap #2 – Going After Possible Goals,* the sweet spot is a number that feels just on the other side of possible, but not so impossible that your nervous system flares up or shuts down. Then as, soon as you set the number for your $ goal, you put on your HILA Hat and unattach from if, when, or how you reach it. The game is not about whether you hit your target, it's about **curiosity** for how far you can get if you focus on leading indicators. And really, it helps you **connect** with and get **creative** and **courageous** about what those leading indicators are and how you go about them.

If your head is swirling a bit about leading and lagging indicators, let me make this more concrete with an example. The first time I played the *90 Day $ Game* was a few months into my business. I was attending Rich Litvin's in-person event for coaches called RLI, and he asked us all to write how much money we'd like to make in the next 90 days on a piece of paper. I wrote $100K. It felt ridiculous. I'd made something like $30K in my first three months in business, and now I was setting a goal to triple that in the following three months! Thankfully nobody needed to know my goal. Or so I thought. Rich asked one of the participants to share his goal. I don't remember what it was, but I know it was fairly low, and didn't satisfy Rich. He turned to me. Cue panic: *F*ck. Now I can't pretend I wrote something more reasonable down.* I took a deep breath and told him my number. Rich was intrigued. We could have done the math I demonstrated above, working backwards from how many one-on-one clients I'd need to enroll at my current prices (leading indicator), and then how many coaching conversations I'd need to have to enroll that many clients (leading indicator), and then how many people I need to invite to coaching conversations … but the math would have told me one thing: I needed to invite, coach, and enroll A LOT of people. Instead, Rich asked me, "What could you offer, and to whom, that a single client would pay you $100K for it?"

I knew that I likely wouldn't go down the route of offering a single client $100K, but the question got my **creative** juices flowing. What else could I offer besides 1:1 coaching? Who do I want to coach and what could I offer them? How might my coaching fees need to adjust? When I got home from the event, I brainstormed all kinds of ideas, including group programs, corporate workshops, and coaching packages that included transformational experiences and travel alongside coaching. Rich had encouraged me in another

IT'S ALL FUN AND GAMES ... NO, REALLY!

part of the event to triple my fees. I knew I wasn't ready for that, either in my level of coaching mastery or in my nervous system, but I did double them. Not only did I get creative about my offerings, but I also leaned into courage to offer free coaching to anyone who was interested. And *that* led me to lean into even more courage and speak about what I was doing in personal conversations and on social media. I wasn't going to create $100K in 90 days if people didn't know about what I was up to in the world!

I didn't hit the $100K goal. If you're thinking, "Oh no! The game didn't work," remember reaching $100K was not the point! I did make ~$66K though, more than double what I had made in my first three months, and for sure it was way more than I would have earned if I'd continued to go about my normal process without creatively and courageously stretching myself. I had more fun than I otherwise would have, too! In fact, one of the most fun parts was designing a "game board" on my whiteboard wall to track my progress. It was a rainbow road. Every thousand dollars, I colored in a brick on the road. And every thousand dollars in proposed fees (lead indicator) became a little pot of gold alongside the road!

I often suggest that my clients play the *90 Day $ Game* when they are first starting their business, but I also sometimes suggest it for clients who are in a rut and need a stretch to juice them up and bring them back into joy-full creation. No matter where you are in business, the *90 Day $ Game* can be a joy-infusion that has the bonus of potentially bringing you a cash infusion too!

Create Your Own Game

If you'd like to create your own game, here are some ideas for getting started.

Design for the Journey Not the Destination.

This may seem counterintuitive. Yes, you want to have a destination in mind. But the whole idea is to make the journey more fun, **creative**, and/or **courageous**. Some questions you might ask yourself:

What would make each step along the journey more joy-full? It might be as simple as tracking them like in *Networking Bingo*. Or it might be tapping into your inner child and giving yourself gold star stickers as you reach particular milestones.

What would make the overall journey more **creative**? Are there alternate routes you can take to the same destination? As I mentioned, when I played the *90 Day $ Game* a few years ago, I expanded my offerings from solely one-on-one coaching to corporate workshops and a group program.

How can you stretch your **courage** muscle? Candace increased the boldness of her requests as she went along in her *Collecting Nos Game*. That helped her realize that no "NO" was as bad as she once thought it was.

Keep your HILA Hat on

Again, the game is all about the journey, so it's key to let go of attachment to the destination. The idea is not to win the game, and it means nothing about you if you don't. Remember, I made $66K of $100K in my first *90 Day $ Game*. What was important was the **creativity** and **courage** it evoked in me, not whether I hit the target.

Make it all up as you go!

Remember our earlier conversations about not needing a Why, What, or How (*Tell Me Why (Ain't Nothing but a Heartache)*, *We Don't Need No Destination!*, *How Do I …*)? Those apply here too. You don't need a fully fleshed-out structure or rules to get playing. Your game can be like a 5-year-old telling a story, full of unformed scenes, nonsensical tangents, and incongruous "and thens."

Pull out your arts and crafts supplies!

Part of the fun I have in playing games is creating a gameboard that delights and excites me. Sure, I could track progress in Excel or in a notebook, but where is the joy in that? We're here to MAXIMIZE our joy. So, pull out your drawing paper and colored pencils. Make a space on your whiteboard. Heck, pull out a piece of wood to etch into or a canvas to paint on if that's your jam. Whatever your medium, make sure it can be put somewhere where you can see it.

A client who is a consultant for nonprofits and NGOs once said in a coaching session, "How can I *play* my way into signing my next client?" I love this question. It's a powerful and joy-full way to create success.

How can you play your way to whatever you want to achieve next?

"IT'S ALL RESEARCH"

I remember the moment my first coach, Caitlin Padgett (who you first met in *Fi Fi Fo Fum ... Plant Some Magic Beans*), said this on a group coaching call. A client was beating herself up for partying a little too hard the night before. The woman was mid-shame spiral when Caitlin stopped her and said something to the effect of, "Let's look at this differently. What if it's all research? What I mean by that is, last night happened. You can't change it. But you can learn something about it. What were the circumstances? Who was around? What were you thinking and feeling? What can you take going forward that will help you recognize your limits in the future?"

I watched as the shame and guilt rose out of Caitlin's client almost as if it was exorcised. With a sense of lightness and curiosity, she became a researcher on the previous night's experience. What had just moments ago been painful suddenly lost its charge. It was brilliant coaching AND a brilliant way to look at the world.

A light bulb went on for me in that moment. I am a scientist and researcher at heart. Between my academic history and my corporate roles, I spent nearly a decade eating, sleeping, and breathing all things data analysis, experimentation, surveys, and interviews. With "It's all research," Caitlin was speaking my language — but in a way I hadn't previously considered.

Since then, "It's all research" as a concept has expanded into much more for me than looking back on past actions to understand what led to them. Being a scientist and researcher is at the foundation of everything I do in my business. It's also a way I create and cultivate joy.

If you're wondering how something that sounds like hard science can relate to joy, let's start with some things that take us away from joy. After a night of partying, Caitlin's client was feeling the shame of her failure to moderate herself. Though she didn't share what her inner voices were saying to her, I can imagine that they were pretty nasty. In her mind, it meant something about her worth — that she'd "f*cked up and she was BAD."

Most of our fears, of failure, rejection, disappointing others, uncertainty, and even success, are about what we'll tell ourselves if they come true. If I fail, it means I'm not good enough. If I'm rejected, I'm unlovable. If I'm successful, I'll have to walk around hiding that I'm a fraud. Those voices in our head can be brutal. Often more so than what anyone outside of us might say.

To shut up those inner voices, we do everything possible to prevent our fears from coming true. That leads us to perfectionism and needing to "get it right" in our heads before we take action. We might sit on putting out a program, waiting for a sign that it's flawless and guaranteed to be a success. We might fret over an approach to something in our business, worried about what happens if we choose wrong.

Whether it's the pressure we put on ourselves prior to taking action or the ways we beat ourselves up for actions that don't work out as planned, we have no room for joy when everything feels high stakes for our self-esteem.

Over the next four conversations, we'll explore ways you can apply "It's all research" to keep out joy-stealing thoughts. We'll also talk about how it can *create* joy by helping you tap into your **curiosity, creativity,** and **courage.**

DATA HATH NO MEANING

"Data hath no meaning."

~ Michael Burgoon (my dad)

I'm not sure *I* ever heard my dad say this phrase, but I've been told by many of his former graduate students that he used it a lot as a professor and PhD advisor, especially when he was teaching. I have no idea where the saying comes from. For all I know, he invented it. Until recently I didn't even know what context he used it in. (I asked my mom, who was also a colleague of his, and learned there is a second part of the phrase ... it makes more sense for how he would have used it, but I prefer the sentence as I remember it).

I've personally adopted "Data Hath No Meaning" as a mantra in my business and life. Let me explain. Humans are meaning-making machines. I mean we are certifiable *experts* at telling ourselves stories about what our experiences mean. If we send a text to someone we have a crush on and they don't answer right away, we might tell ourselves that they aren't interested in us. Or that we're too forward. If we're at a party and we overhear a group of people laughing just after we walked by, we might tell ourselves that they were making fun of us.

Our meaning-making doesn't magically turn off when we're running our businesses. We tell ourselves all kinds of stories about what it means if we fill (or don't fill) a program, sell (or don't sell) a product, sign (or don't sign) a new client, hit (or don't hit) a revenue goal. When we succeed, we tell ourselves it means that we are smart, capable, valuable, creative, good enough. And on the flip side, when we fail, we aren't any of those things. Instead, we're incapable, incompetent, dumb as a box of rocks, unworthy, and certainly not good enough. We can be especially self-critical if we have a high "internal locus of control." That is, we believe that we are mostly responsible for, or in control of, our outcomes (as opposed to external forces like other people, luck, fate, or God being responsible for our situation). For instance, if I think it's 100% "on me" whether a client signs on to work with me, then I'm completely ignoring or discounting any other factors that might lead them to say yes or no. And that means their yes or no is about me — my capabilities as a coach and salesperson — and not anything else. Now my value or self-worth hinges on the decision they make, which ironically, gives all the control to my potential client!

The notion that we are in control of our destiny is baked into our individualistic society. In America this concept is particularly embedded, but it shows up in many other cultures as well. Individualism tells us, "Success is in your hands!" and "If you can't make it to the top, that's on you!" Now, this notion isn't *all* bad. In fact, people who believe they are in control of their outcomes do create more success, take more action, and are more confident in themselves than people who believe external factors are responsible for their outcomes. But, as I have already highlighted, when we completely shoulder the responsibility for our successes and failures, we can quickly make up false narratives about ourselves — and those stories can end up running the show. "I just signed a client. I'm a badass!" can quickly turn into, "I just got a no. I'm a shit coach. I'm a shit salesperson. I'm probably just shitty in general. I'm never going to make it … I might as well give up."

When our stories are in control, we cannot operate from **connection, curiosity, creativity,** or **courage.** In other words, our meaning-making crowds out our joy. This brings me back to my dad's phrase … *data hath no meaning*. A single data point can't tell us much. And depending on what question you are trying to answer with a quantitative approach, it can take hundreds of data points until a clear picture begins to emerge. The concept of collecting data in your business may not be new to you. After all, we live in a data-driven, quantification-obsessed world. But perhaps what will be new to you is what you can consider to be "data."

Everything you do is data.

Every action, nonaction, activity, project, or client. A single LinkedIn post. A single conversation at a conference. A single enrollment conversation with a client. A single unproductive day staring at the computer. Even a single thought or feeling! You might want to read that again because it's a game-changing concept. (At least it was for me.) And, again, a single piece of data carries no meaning. It says nothing about you, your process, or your strategy. Only after you have repeated something many times over can you start looking at the collection of data points for a story. After hundreds of LinkedIn posts, you might notice that certain types of content resonate with your audience. After multiple conversations at conferences and networking events, you may notice that how you talk about what you do isn't landing and could use some tweaks. After dozens of enrollment calls, you can start looking at what might be leading to a string of Nos. After weeks of unproductively staring at the computer, then you might be able to look deeper to make a connection about what is blocking you.

Attention: *Notice that making meaning about a collection of data doesn't mean making meaning about YOU.* Data is objective. It allows you to look at what you might keep doing and what may need a different approach. It doesn't allow you (or anyone for that matter) to judge you or your worth.

You might be wondering, well how much data do I need to collect before I can start looking for patterns? I don't have an answer for that. When it comes to seeing everything as data, it's more of an art than a science. I'm someone who likes to err on the side of making as little meaning as possible until it seems abundantly clear that there is a pattern and that no external circumstances could easily explain what is happening.

The more you put on your proverbial lab coat and operate your business like you're a scientist collecting data, the more you can follow your **curiosity, creativity,** and **courage,** and the less you'll internally lash yourself for a single mistake, misstep, or failure. And *also,* the more you'll come to realize that you are much less in control

DATA HATH NO MEANING

of your outcomes than our culture has taught you to believe. A post on social media can go viral or it can get crickets, and have nothing to do with the content of that post, but instead have everything to do with how the algorithm works or who just happened to share it with their networks. A group program might not fill because it's the middle of summer and people are prioritizing vacations. A revenue drought might be due to a pandemic, war, or economic recession that has people tightening their wallets or investing their money and time differently. We can do our best and the universe will still do what it does.

Data may hath no meaning, but it does "hath" 😉 the ability to create space for joy!

COLLECT SOME DATA

The best way to hone your ability to treat everything like a scientist is to track your actions and notice what feelings come up and what meaning you attach to outcomes. For each activity, note:

- the outcome as succinctly as possible like an experimenter would (success/fail)
- the emotion* that came up as a result of the outcome
- the meaning you made about the outcome (if any), and then, note the real meaning.

Don't skip the step of what you are/were making it mean if you've already reframed. It's important to track any patterns you have in meaning-making along with everything else.

*We'll talk about why tracking the emotion is important for your joy in *Put on Your Lab Coat AND Feel Your Feelings Too.*

DATA HATH NO MEANING

Activity	Outcome (Success/Fail)	Emotion	What I'm Making It Mean	What It Really Means

JOY GUIDES; EXPERIMENT DECIDES

There's a famous research adage that goes: "Theory guides. Experiment decides."[17] Well, that's all well and good for experiments in science, but we're talking business here! I like my version of the maxim (in the conversation title) a bit better 😉. But speaking of science, let's talk about my dad again ...

When I was a kid, I spent a lot of time at my parents' office at the University of Arizona. Behind my dad's door was a coat and hat rack. It held only one item — a lab coat. Just like I have no idea where his saying "data hath no meaning" came from, I don't have a clue where the lab coat came from. Maybe a Halloween costume or a practical joke by his grad students? It's possible I asked him at some point, but if I did, whatever he answered didn't stick. All I knew was that as a professor of communication, he wasn't the kind of doctor who needed a lab coat.

Nowadays I think about that lab coat almost every day in my business. In *Data Hath No Meaning,* I mentioned the idea of putting on your proverbial lab coat. Let me expand on that. One of my favorite ways to be in the joy of collecting data in my business is through designing experiments. And experiments always bring me back to that lab coat. But it wasn't my dad's coat that turned me on to a love of experimentation. It really started with my doctoral work where practically all my research involved running experiments. My love of it grew at Facebook where thousands of experiments were running at any given time to help decide what features ended up in the hands of end users and what exited the app stage right. Facebook tested (and still does!) almost everything you can imagine, from changing the location, text, or color of a button, to large new features like Facebook Stories.

Experimentation can be just as useful for solopreneurs and small businesses as it is for enterprise corporations. And in my opinion, even more joy-full. That's because our experiments don't have to be scientifically rigorous (and it's likely they can't be most of the time). They can, however, be rooted in curiosity about what might happen, creativity in what is being tested and how, and courage to take risks and try things that might fail.

Yet experimentation, as I've found with clients and peers, isn't always baked into business practice. I've seen entrepreneurs get trapped in their heads, trying to figure out the right next step or path, or trying to design the perfect product, service, or experience before taking any action. Life is full of trial and error, but somehow our brains are less forgiving of that in business contexts. Perhaps, as we talked about in *Tell Me Why (Ain't Nothing but a Heartache), We Don't Need No Destination!*, and *How Do I …*, it's because we don't want to waste time, money, or effort going in the wrong direction. And — if we're not seeing our actions as objective data — we don't want to face our feelings (or our Inner Critic's lashings) about failure.

The truth is, it's damned hard to nail *anything* on the first try! And it's even harder to mentally predict what will and won't work. Sometimes we can make a guess, but there's no actual certainty. We can't know for sure what marketing copy is going to resonate with customers unless we put marketing in front of them. We can't know what social media content is going to change people's hearts and minds until we give them something to consume. We can't know what kind of course or program is going to be most useful to people before we run a course or program to try on some of our ideas for size. And that's all just about how other people will feel. What about *our* joy? We can't always know what's going to make us most joy-full to create or do until we try it!

If large enterprise companies can't figure out what will succeed unless they do thousands of experiments, why should we be expected to have all the answers before collecting data?

My client, Danika, was in the early stages of building her coaching practice when she started working with me. One session she came to me with a conundrum about enrolling clients. She was part of both Rich Litvin's and Stacey Boehman's coaching communities. Rich is known for his "Prosperous Coach" approach, which involves giving people deep coaching sessions that last anywhere from 90 minutes to 2 hours as part of enrolling clients. Stacey's approach is a more standard 30-minute "Discovery Call," where the coach gathers some information on the potential client and then talks the person through the different coaching options. In the Discovery Call approach, very little, if any, coaching is done. Danika felt torn. Which approach was right?

I reminded her that "Which approach is right?" was the wrong question. The better question was, "Which approach is right *for me*?" I encouraged her to explore which approach felt best and most aligned with her values, and which ultimately led to the types of clients and client relationships she wanted in her business.

So we designed an experiment: Over her next ten potential client conversations, half would take the Prosperous Coach approach and the other half would take the Discovery Call approach. At the end, she'd decide which *felt* best. Notice I didn't tell her to look at what *worked* best. Ten people, five in each "experimental group" was not enough data in my mind, to know which strategy would be more successful long-term with the types of clients she wanted to work with. What mattered more at this time was what felt the most aligned and joy-full for her. Sure enough, she found her answer. For the time being, the Prosperous Coach approach was going to be Danika's approach.

Doing any experiment requires some courage. Who knows how many of the five clients Danika tested Discovery calls with would have ended up as clients if she'd done all ten calls with the Prosperous Coach approach. Sometimes finding the most joy-full process for you over the long term requires some short-term losses or costs. That can be hard to swallow if you're someone who wants to enroll every potential client or customer that comes through your door. But it's also better than staying stuck in decision paralysis or choosing a strategy without testing it first and only to find what you've chosen is joy-less.

Danika's experiment was numbers-based. That is, I suggested a certain number of potential clients she could have conversations with before determining her enrollment approach going forward. Another way to experiment is with using time.

My client, Jessica, did one of those with me. After leaving one of the biggest corporations in the world and then taking a maternity leave, Jessica had the opportunity to join the C-suite of a tiny start-up. On the table with the offer was the potential for Jessica to become a cofounder of the company several months down the line if she and the founder felt like they were good partners. On paper, it sounded like a dream next step. But as she came off maternity leave, she wasn't quite sure whether this start-up was the right next step *for her*. She'd been toying with the idea of her own start-up or even leaving tech altogether for a different entrepreneurial adventure.

Jessica had spent her entire career chasing promotions and titles, not because she wanted them, but because they told her something (in her mind) about her worth. She had worried constantly about how other people would judge her success. After working with me for several months, she knew that wasn't a healthy way to approach her career and had taken some meaningful steps towards separating her worth from her work. Now with this new role on the table, she worried that if she accepted it, she'd fall back onto old habits and chase the cofounder title as another way to prove herself, rather than truly evaluate whether the company and the title were right for her.

Like with Danika, I suggested an experiment. I hoped that if she was in the mindset of "testing whether it was a fit," she'd worry less about the cofounder possibility and avoid some of the behaviors around proving herself that were so familiar. I also imagined that it would help her try new leadership styles and develop skills (like focusing more on strategy than execution) with less pressure. The founder wanted to wait until Jessica was at the company for six months before evaluating the possibility of bringing her on as cofounder. That seemed like an excellent time frame to work with — long enough to deeply immerse herself in the company, but not long enough that it felt like too large a commitment.

Framing Jessica's time at the start-up as an experiment was a huge success. It allowed her to show up with curiosity: "Which aspects of this role do I like? Which do I not? Which aspects of this company and this time do I like? Which do I not?" It allowed her to step into leadership and strategic thinking, and to discover that those were natural strengths. We checked in regularly about how the experiment was going. We'd make sure she wasn't being sucked into old stories and operating from fear. We'd look at what data supported her staying at the company long-term and what data suggested otherwise. On occasion I would ask her questions like, "What else would you need to find out in order for this experiment to give you a conclusive yes or no to continuing on?" and "At what point would the data be so conclusive, even in these initial six months, that continuing on could not possibly change the outcome?" At the six-month mark, she didn't have enough data, and neither did the founder. So she agreed to a three-month extension. Again, we looked at what data she needed to collect to have an answer. Ultimately, she came to a joy-full decision, one rooted in data and self-connection, that she wanted to head in a different direction.

The beauty of an experiment is that you set out a specific number of actions or a specific time-frame — nothing you are doing is forever. You can wait until the end of the experiment to draw conclusions, but you can also assess along the way whether the data is leaning so far one way or another that it makes sense not to continue.

Take a look at activities or projects that could benefit from you designing an experiment. You can let your joy (or pursuit of it) guide what experiments you try, and let the data decide what activities or projects you ultimately stick with.

IT'S AN 'EXPERIMENT'

In *Joy Guides; Experiment Decides* we talked about the joy of designing experiments to help us make decisions in business. We don't have to run actual experiments to take advantage of experimentation. We can view each action we take as an experiment, even if it's not part of a formal experiment (like Danika did to decide on her approach to enrolling clients and Jessica did to try on the idea of being a cofounder and strategic leader).

You might be thinking, "Wait, Erin, didn't you say everything we do is *data*? Now you're saying everything is an *experiment*. What's the difference?"

When I say everything is data (see *Data Hath No Meaning*), I mean that you can't draw any conclusions from a single action. You don't know why it was or wasn't successful. And data certainly makes no value judgments about who you are as a person. Seeing everything as data is a mindset shift around the *outcome*. When I say everything is an experiment, I mean that no action, activity, project, or program has to be polished or perfect. Ever. And certainly not on the first try.

Seeing everything you do as an experiment is more about the process than outcome.

Your biggest opportunity for joy, in my opinion, is when you see everything as an experiment AND as data. You can lean into **curiosity, creativity,** and **courage** in every stage of a process or action.

One of my favorite examples of leaning into the mindset of "It's an experiment" comes from my colleague, Abbey Gibb. Webinars and masterclasses were a bread-and-butter strategy for Abbey, an Emmy-winning journalist-turned-media and business mentor, as she quickly grew her business to 7-figures. Until she and I met, she'd never considered that she could run a masterclass *her way*.

She'd been taught strategies and tactics, and because they'd worked, she never questioned them. She'd also never asked herself whether her masterclasses brought her joy.

Abbey heard me talk about the Lab Coat concept enough times that she decided to try it for herself. She had an upcoming masterclass and instead of following the formulas and rules she normally adhered to, she let herself treat it as an experiment to see what would happen if she designed it based on questions like: "What would be fun for me?", "What would be most connective for me and for the people who attend?", and "What would feel like 'That's so Abbey?'" She ended up designing a masterclass that was altogether different from her usual. For one, instead of trying to pack as many people as possible into a Zoom room, she limited the number of participants so that she could make it much more intimate and interactive. She knew that by running it with fewer people she might make less money than she had in other masterclasses. That, for her, was a risk she was willing to take in exploring her joy.

Shortly after the masterclass, we were on a Zoom call together. She gushed. It was the most fun she'd ever had in her business. She wasn't sure what the financial outcome would be, or how it would compare to previous masterclasses, but that didn't matter to her. From now on, she was only going to run webinars and masterclasses *her way*, with her joy front and center. (And I suspect that was the start of her doing everything in her business that way.) She's now turning that masterclass content into a book. I am curious if the idea of a book would have come to her had she not leaned into her joy first …

After running an experiment with her masterclass, Abbey could have decided, "Yep, this is how I'll run masterclasses from now on." But I encouraged her to see every masterclass from now on as an experiment. There is no end point where you've perfected your craft and you never change anything ever again. You might as well give yourself permission, over and over again, to test new ideas and not have them all work out. The minute you tell yourself something is "final," you risk putting unnecessary pressure on yourself. There's no joy in that!

[If you're questioning whether *everything* can really be an experiment and that there are never any finished products, I'll use this book as an example. You may see it as a finished product because it's in your hands. I see it as an experiment. The format is unconventional. I know it brought me immense joy to write and format a book in the way my brain thinks, but will it be successful? Will it resonate with readers? Will it accomplish all the things I hope it does? I don't know. It's an experiment!]

PUT ON YOUR LAB COAT AND FEEL YOUR FEELINGS TOO

Seeing our actions as both data collection and as experiments can create space for joy. We can sink into our curiosity and creativity, be more courageous in what we try, and pursue things that feel deeply connected to who we are and how we work. By stripping out some of the anxiety, fear, and pressure that we put on ourselves to be perfect (because after all, failure *means* something about us, right?) there is more room to tap into and cultivate joy. Taking on the mindset of a scientist can be a bit paradoxical, though. Collecting data asks us to be an impartial, emotionless observer. But there's also no joy in being emotionless. It's not possible for us to just get rid of our negative emotions and only keep the positive ones. Our capacity to experience joy is directly related to our capacity to experience pain. So if you want to expand your joy tank, you also need to expand every other emotional tank too!

What gives? How can we need to be objective scientists to feel joy AND at the same time, need to feel all our feelings in order to feel joy? Can they coexist? Yes, they can. That is the paradox. Or at least what appears to be a paradox.

It's best explained through an example, so let's talk about my friend, Inés Ruiz. Inés is the CEO and founder of ELEInternacional, an online school and certification program for Spanish Language teachers across the globe. She grew her business quickly, from low six figures to seven figures in a matter of a couple of years. One of her superpowers is putting on her proverbial lab coat and taking lots of action. A few years ago, she called me for a catch-up. I could tell immediately that she was feeling down. She explained that she had just run a webinar for a new product she was selling, and though she ran webinars often and usually had great attendance, this one had far fewer people show up than she hoped. On top of that, she hadn't made a single sale. She couldn't remember the last time this happened.

I could hear the disappointment and sadness in her voice, but I could also hear that she was trying to stuff down her emotions. She then said something to the effect of, "A good entrepreneur doesn't get caught in their feelings. I know I was trying something new and that doesn't always work. I should remember it's just one webinar. It's just a data point."

We were having this conversation long before joy was in my vocabulary, but what intuitively came out of me in that moment shaped my views on this lab coat paradox.

"Inés, it's okay. *And* … it sucks."

I went on to say, "You get to acknowledge and feel your feelings. Disappointment. Sadness. Frustration. Don't try to stuff it all down. Of course it's good to recognize that it's just a data point and you can't really know why there were fewer people and no sales today. Yes, you tried something different and that could have been why. But it absolutely could've been that it's a nice summer day and people didn't want to be on the computer. Or maybe it was a fluke and if you try again next week, you'll get a completely different result. But you don't stop being a person with feelings when this stuff happens."

Essentially, I was telling Inés to feel her feelings fully AND to not make any meaning out of the lower attendance and zero sales. When we collect data to remove emotionality from our actions, what we really want to do is remove the meaning-making thoughts and feelings (many of which are self-critical). There's a big difference between being disappointed in an outcome that didn't go your way and being disappointed in yourself (or even beating yourself up!). It was clear to me that Inés was experiencing the former — disappointment in the outcome — but she'd picked up a belief that all emotions were problematic and bad for business.

You might be thinking, "Well Erin, if she's caught up in her feelings, won't that stop her from moving forward?" Likely, not. Our emotional states are quite short-lived, lasting from a few minutes to a few hours. Rarely does an emotional state linger longer than a day. And if it does, that's certainly something to look at more deeply. But when we allow ourselves to feel our emotions fully, they dissipate, usually even more quickly than if we try to get rid of them by overriding them or stuffing them down. In fact, not feeling our emotions can lead to depression, lower self-esteem, stress, and physical illness. For Inés, feeling her feelings about the webinar was quite healthy … and great for filling up her joy tank!

You're allowed to have feelings about your successes and failures.

Back to our paradox. You can feel joy and celebration when something goes well. You can feel sadness, disappointment, frustration, anger, or any other emotion when something doesn't go as well as you'd hoped. The more you can feel your feelings, no matter the situation, the more you'll expand your joy tank. But you'll start to leak your joy when you buy into meaning-making thoughts and feelings about what those successes or failures say about you or your business.

In the exercise in *Data Hath No Meaning*, I included a column for emotion. Now that you've read this conversation, you know that it's important to make note of these emotions so that you can allow yourself to feel them independently of any meaning-making your brain wants to create. And you may notice that once you remove the meaning from something, the emotion changes. For instance, if I catch myself lashing myself for a failure to enroll a client, the predominant emotion might be anger towards myself. Once I remove any stories I'm making up about myself, I might just feel a little bummed out that I won't get to work with that person. If given the choice between being a little bummed and trying to be a feelingless robot in my business, I'll choose being a little bummed every day of the week!

NEVER HIKE IN THE BUSINESS WILDERNESS ALONE

Entrepreneurship can be lonely as hell. And yet for some reason, we believe we have to do it (mostly) alone. This is a quick recipe for keeping our joy out. We are social creatures — we need connection and support for our well-being. We also can't see outside ourselves. We all have blind spots and limits to our perspective. Some of the best creativity can come out of other people seeing something that we can't.

Logically, we know we can't do this thing called business alone. But, it's easy to catch ourselves resisting support. Or being highly calculated about what we allow ourselves to seek and receive support on. Like when we don't allow ourselves to use our maps app anymore after a few days in a new city. After all, we should know where we are going by now, right?

Why do we do this to ourselves?

One of the hallmarks of our culture (especially for those of us in the United States) is a belief that's rooted in white supremacy, toxic capitalism, and rugged individualism: If we can't do it all by ourselves, there is something wrong with us. (We also glorify the folks who seem, at least to our eyes, to be able to.) We tell ourselves when we can't pull it off all on our own that we're not capable or competent, and ultimately, not good enough. We believe that we don't deserve to be an entrepreneur and that people will find out we're a fraud if we admit to needing help. Underneath this all is a fear that we'll have to face ourselves and our own self-loathing for the ways we've "failed." Ouch!

When we buy into these lies, we contribute to our own loneliness by denying ourselves access to full support. And really, it's a self-fulfilling prophecy … we don't ask for the exact or full support we need, and then we don't get the help we need, and then we reinforce our belief that we aren't good enough. In what becomes a vicious cycle, we become even less likely to ask for help.

You can choose to continue going alone or being calculated about what support you get. You can even be quite successful. But is that the most joy-full path?

In these next two conversations, we'll explore various ways other people can help you fill your joy tank.

FRODO AND HIS MERRY BAND OF TRAVELERS

Raise your hand if you resonated with the last conversation: You know you can't do this thing called business alone, but you secretly believe you're supposed to. Or some part of you believes that a *true* solopreneur or small business CEO who is smart, capable, and creative enough doesn't really need personal help or support. Now, I'm not talking about flying solo to the degree that you don't hire anyone *in* your business. Depending on the size and nature of your business, you may not need much more than a virtual assistant, or you might need an entire team. The type of support I'm talking about is at the peer, coach, or mentorship level.

You can't see me right now, but I'm raising my hand. I used to believe that if I couldn't build and run a business on my own, I had no business being in business. Granted, it wasn't a completely black-and-white thought. Part of me saw the merit of coaches and peer circles — heck, I invested nearly six figures in my first year of business in three coaches, two of whom also came with a community of fellow coaches. But despite having access to support, I couldn't entirely shake the belief that I was supposed to figure it all out on my own. I made sure my peers never saw what was really going on in my mind and heart. I felt ashamed showing weakness to my coaches. Anything I brought to coaching and peer circles was something safe enough that wouldn't conflict with my belief that good entrepreneurs are self-sufficient.

I was somewhat surprised when I realized that the "go alone" belief was secretly running the show. I grew up with two academic parents and was in academia as a PhD student myself. Almost nothing in academia is done alone. Whether it's coming up with research ideas, designing and executing experiments, or writing academic articles, everything is done in collaboration. There are occasionally single-author papers, but they aren't necessarily held in higher regard than multi-author papers. As a student, I had the mentorship, guidance, and collaboration of my advisor, and I also collaborated with other grad students and professors at my school (University of Texas) and professors from other institutions. It would have never occurred to me that a successful academic career was a solo endeavor.

Another part of me, though, was not at all surprised to uncover the "go alone" belief. As I've talked about again and again, it's woven into the fabric of our individualistic, meritocratic society, particularly here in the United States. Doing something completely on your own carries a badge of honor. We praise people who have "pulled themselves up from their bootstraps" and we denigrate those who need assistance as weak, lazy, and stupid. In some business circles, any form of coaching or mentorship is stigmatized. A 2021 "Tech Crunch" article states, "Founders are resistant to hiring a coach themselves because they're worried about what their investors and board will think of them. They tell themselves: 'If I were normal, and good enough, I wouldn't need one.'"[18]

In my conscious mind, I recognized that I couldn't do it alone. I knew I needed guidance and education on being a coach and business owner. But operating below the surface was, "You're the CEO. You're the sole guide and director of your business." While *technically* true, that belief limited what I thought a coach, mentor, or peer could be useful for. The big vision for my business? Up to me. What I offered as services and programs? Up to me. Navigating some of the fears and challenges I faced as I built the business … most definitely up to me.

What did I get from these coaches, then? I absorbed a lot from their teachings and in watching them coach other people. With my one-on-one coach, I was cautious for a while, asking tactical rather than vulnerable questions about "How to do X," or getting feedback on things I'd already thought about and/or created. I wouldn't have dared come to her with, "Hey, I'd like some help brainstorming my next group program."

If I had reminded myself that the CEOs of some of the biggest corporations are almost never on their own — they almost always have advisors, coaches, *and* boards of directors — I might have had a different viewpoint. But I also heard that nagging inner voice reminding me, "If you can't do some of these things on your own, you shouldn't be in business." Thankfully I discovered early on (still in that first year of coaching while working with my three coaches) that a highly individualistic part of me was in the driver's seat.

When I started unpacking the belief that I shouldn't need help and instead leaned into support for all the things I felt I had to do alone, I realized it was a key to running a joy-full business. As I allowed myself to open up to coaches and peers in my community, I felt some of the same aliveness and fun that I used to experience when collaborating in the academic world. When I let my mentors fully help me, and when I leaned into peers for everything from brainstorming to emotional support, I noticed that they joy-fully engaged too. Who knew that me asking for help could be a source of joy for others!?

Nowadays, I always have one-on-one support from a coach or therapist (sometimes both) and I'm always part of a community. Who supports me and what community I participate in shifts with my needs, but one thing is constant: I'm never hiking in my business wilderness alone. I lean on my people for everything from strategy and tactics to deep emotional and nervous system support.

In a world that sees needing assistance as a sign of weakness, I've come to believe that the real weakness is flying solo. Not a personal weakness, but a weak position. There's a reason academia is a collaborative space. The biggest scientific breakthroughs have all come when people have pooled their resources — emotional, mental, and physical. I believe a similar thing can be true in our businesses: we create our greatest impact and most brilliant ideas when we allow ourselves to benefit from the wisdom, experience, and support of others.

> *"If you want to go fast, go alone;*
> *if you want to go far, go together."*
>
> ~ Origin unknown

I've seen and heard this quote many times in my circles. The quote as a whole doesn't exactly land for me since I don't think fast and far are mutually exclusive. But I do love the last part: "If you want to go far, go together." I'd even add, "If you want to go far *joy-fully*, go together."

Speaking of far, I've heard being in business likened to Joseph Campbell's hero's journey[19] in my circles. Almost all storytelling, from ancient myths to today's blockbusters, follow the hero's journey pattern where a main character sets out on a challenge, faces many obstacles along the way, and emerges victorious. One of the hallmarks of the hero's journey is that the hero never does it alone. He/she/they always have a mentor and a merry band of fellow travelers. When I think of the concept of "never hike alone," I think of *The Lord of the Rings*. After all, the journey from the Shire to Mordor *was* a hike! Frodo, in saving Middle Earth from Sauron, sets off with Gandalf (his mentor) and his cheery friends Pippin, Sam, and Merry. Along the way, Aragorn, Legolas, Gimli, and Boromir join him. In the end, each character had a role to play in helping Frodo be successful.

Whether you see your business as a hike through the wilderness (like I do) or a hero's journey through Middle Earth, you will have more joy, and perhaps go farther than you thought possible, if you commit to never hiking alone. That could mean a one-on-one coach, a group program, a paid community, or simply gathering like-minded peers on a regular basis. (At times I've had all of them!) Investing time, money, and relational energy in your business and yourself is not only a source of joy in itself, but it's also a way to be supported in keeping joy front and center in everything you do.

RUNNING BUDDIES

Did you know there are apps for finding a running buddy? A simple Google search also brings up dozens of articles on where and how you can find the perfect running partner. And, if you're someone who is not yet convinced that you need a running buddy, there are dozens of articles on that too — all about the benefits of having someone running alongside you.

Why the hell am I talking about running in a book on joy-full AF business? I used to be a casual runner, and I see a lot of parallels between running and entrepreneurship. The most obvious is that it's a solo sport. Similarly, entrepreneurship can be or feel like a solo endeavor, whether you're a "company of one" or leader of a small operation. A less obvious, but perhaps more important, parallel is that entrepreneurship is something we need to take at our own pace. We have to learn to run our own race.

Still, even though runners need to learn their pace and run their own race, running buddies are quite common. That's why there are apps and Google articles dedicated to it. Regrettably, the same is not true for entrepreneurship. There are no apps for entrepreneurial "running buddies." I have not yet found any articles on how to find one or what the benefits are of having them. And in case you're wondering how this is different from the support we talked about in *Frodo and His Merry Band of Travelers*, let me draw the distinction. A coach in your business is akin to a running coach. Runners who are dedicated to racing often have coaches *and* running buddies. Your merry band of travelers — your peer community — most often is a place where you share with others *about* your business and get support. It's not always a place where people are actively working on their businesses in real-time together. There are many ways to "never hike alone" in my mind. Running buddies are just an additional option to the ones we've already talked about.

What exactly is a running buddy in the business context? We are all running our own race and at our own pace, but sometimes we are on a similar course as some of our peers. For instance, you may be actively trying to grow your social media following and find that you have peers in the thick of that too. Or maybe you're writing a TEDx talk or book and have peers doing the same. You could certainly meet with your peers every week or two to talk *about* the process. Or if you're part of an online community, you might consider reaching out for support when you have a challenge. Both of those options follow the more traditional model I talked about in *Frodo and His Merry Band of Travelers*. Consider for a moment, if you had a running buddy or two, you'd be *in it* together, sharing your goals (like 'post once daily on social media' or 'write 100 words a day') and checking in with one another on progress. You could cheer each other on, support each other when things are challenging, or even simply have space to vent (one of my favorites parts of having running buddies).

My running buddies have been a huge help for me building a social media presence. When I tried to "run alone," holding myself accountable to posting and growing my network was difficult for me. I lost energy and motivation without someone in it with me. I'd make excuses not to post. I'd get lost in perfectionism or would talk myself out of posting certain things. It all makes sense, as I'm more able to accomplish my goals when I have external accountability. (According to Gretchen Rubin's in *The Four Tendencies*[20] — another not-so-scientific assessment that I still find to be a useful lens — I am an *Obliger*. Whereas some people need zero accountability to meet their goals, and others actively rebel against accountability, *Obligers* thrive with it. Turns out, I'm in good company: about 41% of people are *Obligers*.)

In late 2020, Varian Brandon, a colleague who had built an engaged and loyal following on Facebook, put out a program for people who wanted to unlock their authentic expression online. Initially, I wasn't going to join the program. At the time, I was sporadically posting on Facebook. I had done 90 days of Facebook lives (that I first mentioned in *Uncomfortable Versus Unsafe*) over a year earlier — I knew how to authentically express myself. I could even do it in a stream-of-conscious style live! I couldn't imagine paying Varian to help me with social media. (Of course, in true *Obliger* fashion, just because I knew how to do it didn't mean I could hold myself accountable to doing it!) Then I found out that two of my other colleagues, Matt and Andy, and my coach at the time, Christina, were joining. Now *that* was a compelling reason to jump in! I messaged Varian to sign me up.

The program had us posting multiple times a day. There was a Facebook group for everyone in the program, and alongside that, Andy, Matt, Christina, and I had a highly active text thread. It was so fun to share things, both on Facebook and over text, like "Wow, this post blew up!" and "Oh my gosh, that was vulnerable to share!" It was even nice to talk about the program itself: "Why do you think we're being asked to post this?" "What are you liking so far and what would you change?"

As soon as the program was over, we went our separate ways. Without my running buddies, my energy waned. I went back to sporadic posting, though it was probably slightly less sporadic than before the program. I even considered giving up social media. Until another opportunity for me to have some running buddies game along.

Just like the first program, I had no intention of joining a social media-based program. I'd been following the leader, Simone Seol, on Instagram for months, but never felt compelled to look into her Joyful Marketing Program. (You'd think I would have been all over something with 'Joyful' in the name, right?) Then I saw a colleague, David, post on his Instagram that he was in the program. Soon I found out two other colleagues, Allison and Christina (the same Christina who did Varian's program with me), had also just joined. I knew immediately that joining Joyful Marketing with these folks was the key to making my social media joy-full again. I proverbially ran (not walked 😊) to Simone's website and joined the program.

Like in Varian's program, Allison, Christina, and I had a text thread where we shared our experience of going through the

"Garbage Post Challenge" — to create 100 pieces of content in 30 days. My energy for social media returned in full force. So much was pouring out of me that I did 120 posts in the 30-day window. (In case you're thinking, holy moly that's a lot, anything with words counted as a post. If I posted a Story on Instagram about my dog with any caption at all, it qualified per the rules of the game.)

I don't need, or even want, running buddies for everything I do. But when I do, they help me do all sorts of things I might have struggled to complete on my own. That doesn't make me weak or wrong. Running buddies also take me *further* than I would have gone on my own — adding to my energy and joy (and therefore stamina) in whatever it is we're doing. It's fun to see where we each end up. And even without their motivation benefits, running buddies are simply joy-full to have with me on the journey — a solid reminder that we're never alone.

If the idea of having a running buddy as part of filling your joy tank is intriguing, I highly recommend first taking *The Four Tendencies* assessment. It will help you understand how you operate in regards to motivation and how running buddies (or which running buddies) might best work for you in the context of your business.

KEEP YOUR JOY TANK TOPPED OFF

Joy is vital fuel in your business. Having a full tank provides the resources and the resilience you need to endure the ebbs and flows that every business experiences. No business operates consistently. It's natural to go through times when nothing feels like it's working, or you're not totally sure where your next client is coming from. And it's just as normal to go through times when everything seems to work seamlessly, and clients and customers are abundant. As much as we'd like to be fully in control of the success of our businesses, and have clear predictability and consistency, all of these ideas are an illusion. COVID-19 was an extreme example of this, showing us that at any time, the entire world can come to an abrupt halt.

Joy can buffer us from the natural ebbs and flows in business, and those of the world. It's not just our businesses that are impacted by global pandemics, European wars, political upheaval, inflation, and stock market fluctuations. *We are affected as humans, too.* Our mental and emotional well-being depends on the context we live in, from running our businesses, to our personal lives, to national and world events.

Joy is the fuel and we need a full tank.

When I say joy is fuel and we need a full tank, it's not like gasoline in a car. You don't run the tank down, waiting until you're down to fumes and on the verge of crisis to fill back up again. Even if you're one of those highly conscientious folks who fills up before their tank reaches ¼ left, that just won't do for your joy tank.

Joy is more like water in our human body. We need lots of water in order to survive. But we're not supposed to just drink when we're thirsty. In fact, if we guzzle water after letting ourselves get parched (like after a day at the beach), we can feel ill afterwards. The more sustainable, healthy way to consume water is to drink it regularly and keep our hydration tank full. That's how I want you to think about your joy — it's a tank to keep as full as possible. That way you can draw on your joy tank without completely depleting yourself when things aren't going as well as you'd like or when the world seems like too much.

I hope that you've come to understand throughout these pages that it's not toxic positivity to seek joy. It's not burying your head in the sand either. Remember, we can experience joy alongside all kinds of other emotions. You can feel frustrated that nothing's working right now. You can feel anxious that your cash flow isn't as steady as you'd like it to be. You can feel downright angry and devastated by the impact of COVID-19, the Russian invasion of Ukraine, or the treatment of black people in America. *And* you can still find moments and pockets of joy to fill you up.

You can keep your joy tank topped off in multiple ways. I've given you several ideas in these pages — like creating games, planting Magic Beans, putting on your HILA hat, or wearing your lab coat — but there are an endless number of ways available to you. I make a regular practice of intentionally infusing joy into my work. Every Monday, I host a Zoom session called Joy-Full Biz Intentions Setting where I share journal prompts that help me and attendees plan more joy into their week. I also maintain a daily practice.

Every morning, I run through five questions:

First I ask, "Do I need rest?"

Did this question stop you in your tracks? Our first instinct when wanting more of something is to add more things to our to-do list. What if filling up on joy requires us to do less? And what would life be like if we asked ourselves, in any circumstance, what we can do less of before asking what we need to do more of?

If the answer is yes ... I do not pass go. I do not collect $200. I figure out what I can cut out of my day to give myself time to re-energize. I also look at what personal joys might feel like rest that day, like going on a long walk or playing basketball in my driveway.

If the answer is no ... I then turn to the four ingredients of joy:

What can I get curious about today?

What do I want to create today?

What act of courage can I take today?

How can I create a connection to myself or to someone else?

When I answer, I try to get as specific as possible. On days when joy feels difficult — when I want to throw in the towel on my business or I'm mad at the state of the world — I make sure all my answers are about the tiniest actions possible. What is a tiny curiosity? A tiny thing I can create? A tiny act of courage? A tiny moment of connection?

A tiny curiosity might be trying a new question or tool with a client. A tiny creation might be an Instagram Story. A tiny act of courage might be turning off my computer an hour early. A tiny act of connection might be sending a text to a colleague saying, "Hey, I'm thinking about you. I hope your day is going well!"

When I focus on these four ingredients — whether they are four separate activities, or one that includes all four ingredients — every day, my joy tank not only overflows, but it also expands its capacity.

Are you treating your joy like gas for the car or like water for your body? What could you do weekly or daily to cultivate more joy? Certainly, you could use the questions I ask myself, but perhaps it would be more joy-full to create your own!

Epilogue: What Happens If We All Follow Our Joy?

*"Everyone can dance;
they just have their own rhythm and style."*

~ Patti Dizon

Growing up, I spent two weeks of every summer at Camp-Al-Gon-Quian in northern Michigan. (This was the camp I mentioned in ~~Love~~ Joy and Basketball.) It was a traditional YMCA camp with activities like sailing, canoeing, archery, and arts and crafts. To me, camp was the happiest place on earth. It was the only place, at the time, where I could be completely myself. I could play sports all day with the boys and nobody would bat an eye. I could be completely out of touch with current (feminine) fashion and actually fit in with many others who were equally out of touch. Though many campers knew each other from middle or high school, my schoolmates were thousands of miles away in Arizona. That meant I could experiment with and explore my identity (including thinking about whether I was gay). I could express myself in ways I would be shy about elsewhere. And I could make new friends away from social hierarchies.

I felt true belonging and acceptance at camp. From the moment I showed up there at 11 years old, I was shown unconditional love by campers and staff. As each year passed, that love grew stronger as I built relationships with people who came back year after year. Patti Dizon was one of those counselors. One evening when I was about 14, she and I were talking about the camp dance that was about to start. I was anxious. In my mind, I didn't know how to dance. Or if I did, I certainly wasn't very good at it. I was worried that I was about to embarrass myself in front of everyone. Without a beat she replied, "Oh Er-Bear (still her nickname for me), *everyone* can dance; they just have their own rhythm and style." To this day, it's one of the most profound things I've ever been told.

Patti was right. Everyone was so full of joy that night as they all danced their own dance. I didn't even think to look at whether they were "doing it right." (Okay maybe I did look a *little* bit. I was 14 after all!) She was also right about more than dance. At Camp Al-Gon-Quian, everyone was loved for exactly who they were, no matter what rhythm they were walking, running, or dancing to. They were even *encouraged* to bring out who they were in full force. Camp wasn't just a happy place — it was a joy-full place.

I've said for several years that I'm on a secret mission to make the world like summer camp. At least like Camp Al-Gon-Quian was in the late 90s. I've come to believe through writing *Joy-Full AF* that the key to achieving that mission is for all of us to follow our joy in everything we do, including business.

What does that look like in the business world? It starts with recognizing that Patti's advice holds true. We can all run successful businesses, and the most joy-full and sustainable way to do it is with our own rhythm and style. When we deeply **connect** with who we are, what lights us up, how we tick, and what our bodies are telling us ... when we let our natural **curiosity** take over and allow ourselves to play, experiment, and wonder what might happen next ... when we tap into our **creative** reservoirs to create inspired and innovative ideas ... and when we **courageously** go after what our hearts and souls most deeply desire ... we create success and fulfillment that keeps us going through the inevitable ebbs and flows. I believe that the more each of us follows our joy — and really the more we get to deeply know ourselves — the more we can create a new business culture that eschews the hustle and grind lifestyle, go-big-or-go-home mentality, and 10-step formulas for success, in favor of self-trust, authenticity, and individuality.

As I've written, following our joy can be uncomfortable. Often it requires that we question the advice and mentorship we've been soaking up as truth. It means confronting long-held beliefs and butting up against white supremacy culture, patriarchy, and internalized capitalism. And, as we look inward for answers in a society that has taught us to look outward, it means getting to know, like, and trust ourselves on levels more deeply than ever.

Choosing joy is an act of resistance

Even when we commit to our joy, we'll inevitably find ways to lose it. I'll be the first one to tell you that after all this exploration of joy, I *still* do too. The more aware we are of it happening, the sooner we can plug up the leaks. We also need to be intentional about choosing to infuse *more* joy into our work, especially when deadlines, priorities, and business challenges tempt us to put joy on the backburner. Putting joy first is not always easy. But I hope that after reading *Joy-Full AF*, you feel more equipped than before to do so.

May you chase joy and find that success chases you. May you seek joy and find *you* (and vice versa). And may we all find ourselves in business a world (and even broader world) that feels like summer camp.

Yours Joy-fully,

Erin

Resources

1 Robert A Emmons, "Joy: An introduction to this special issue," *The Journal of Positive Psychology* 15, no.1 (2020): 1-4. DOI: 10.1080/17439760.2019.1685580.

2 Samin Nostrat. *Salt, Fat, Acid, Heat: Mastering the Elements of Good Cooking* (New York, NY: Simon & Shuster, 2017).

3 Rob Bell, "An Introduction to Joy," July 18, 2020, YouTube video, 1:19:42, https://www.youtube.com/watch?v=sA7LmEn3xyc.

4 Simone Seol, "The Price of a Joyful Business with Caryn Gillen," *Joyful Marketing*, March 8, 2022, podcast audio, https://www.simonegraceseol.com/podcast/joyful-business-caryn-gillen.

5 Karen Walrond, *The Lightmaker's Manifesto: How to Work for Change Without Losing Your Joy* (Minneapolis, MN: Broadleaf Books, 2021).

6 Richard Schwartz, *No Bad Parts: Healing Trauma and Restoring Wholeness With the Internal Family Systems Model* (Boulder, CO: Sounds True, 2021)

7 Katherine Gustafson, "The Percentage of Businesses That Fail and How to Boost Your Chances of Success," Lending Tree, May 2, 2022, https://www.lendingtree.com/business/small/failure-rate/.

8 Gay Hendricks, *The Big Leap: Conquer Your Hidden Fear and Take Life to the Next Level* (New York, NY: Harper Collins, 2010).

9 Steve Chandler and Rich Litvin, *The Prosperous Coach: Increase Income and Impact for You and Your Clients* (Anna Maria, FL: Maurice Bassett, 2013).

10 "White Supremacy Culture Characteristics", https://www.whitesupremacyculture.info/characteristics.html.

11 Chip Heath and Dan Heath, *The Power of Moments* (London, UK: Random House, 2017).

12 Jonathan Fields, "Sparketypes Assessment: Discover What Makes You Come Alive", https://sparketype.com/.

13 Mark J. Silverman, *Only 10s 2.0: Confront Your To-Do List and Transform Your Life* (Mark J. Silverman, 2020).

14 Brené Brown, "The Power of Vulnerability", TEDxHouston, online video, 20:23, https://www.ted.com/talks/brene_brown_the_power_of_vulnerability?language=en.

15 David Eagleman, *Livewired: The Inside Story of the Ever-Changing Brain* (New York, NY: Vintage Books, 2020).

16 Brené Brown, "The Inside Story of the Ever-Changing Brain with David Eagleman," *Unlocking Us*, December 2, 2020, podcast audio, https://brenebrown.com/podcast/brene-with-david-eagleman-on-the-inside-story-of-the-ever-changing-brain/.

17 "Izaak Mauritis Kolthoff and Modern Analytical Chemistry," American Chemical Association, https://en.wikipedia.org/wiki/Izaak_Kolthoff.

18 Ariane de Bonvoison, "Investors and business leaders: It's time to take coaching mainstream," Tech Crunch, March 25, 2021, https://techcrunch.com/2021/03/25/investors-and-business-leaders-its-time-to-take-coaching-mainstream/.

19 "Hero's Journey", Wikipedia, https://en.wikipedia.org/wiki/Hero%27s_journey.

20 Gretchen Rubin, The Four Tendencies: The Indispensable Personality Profiles That Reveal How to Make Your Life Better (and Other People's Lives Better, Too) (New York, NY: Harmony Books, 2017). The Four Tendencies Quiz: https://quiz.gretchenrubin.com/.

Acknowledgments

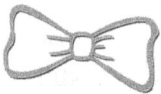

I have been fortunate to not have to hike alone in writing this book. I've had some of the most incredible Gandalfs, merry bands of travelers, and running buddies that a human could ask for.

To Simone Seol: I have only experienced "take your breath away" joy a few times in my life, and one of those was reading your foreword. It beautifully captured the power of joy, the message of the book, and who I am, while also embodying who you BE as a leader and coach. I am honored that you agreed to be a part of this book and will be forever reminded that the best part of the "Collecting Nos" game is the feeling of surprise and excitement when someone says yes!

To my clients: I am profoundly grateful and honored to have walked alongside each of you on your journeys. You have trusted me with your hopes, dreams, desires, fears, vulnerabilities, and challenges. You have let me see, hold, and support all of you — the parts you love and the parts you don't. And you have generously allowed me to share your stories in the hope of helping others along the journey. You are the reason my work is joy-full AF.

To Patti M. Hall: You have been much more than a book coach and story builder for me over the last two years. From "a book about AND" to The Ten Essentials to *Joy-Full AF*, you were steadfast in helping me navigate the twists and turns, and ups and downs of the book-writing wilderness. You believed in me when I didn't. You refused to give up when I thought, "No, this time the joy really is gone. I'm quitting." Your heart, generosity, tenacity, and grit are unmatched. Words will never fully capture my gratitude.

To the Story House crew, Ken Bechtel and Tim Snell: You were my much-needed running buddies for the first several months of book writing. I am so grateful that Patti brought us together and that we could go through the early mess of "what am I writing a book on?" in good company. Book writing can be a lonely endeavor, but being "in it" with you made it so much more joy-full.

To Mark Silverman, Shelley Paxton, Mandy Lehto, Erin Hatzikostas, and Catherine Hammond: You are some of the most soulful, big-hearted, and brilliant humans I know. Thank you for sharing your wisdom and experience in writing and publishing your books. But even more so, thank you for being cheerleaders and champions of me and my work. I am grateful to not only call each of you colleagues but also soul friends.

To my coaches and business mentors over the last few years, Christina Berkley, Rich Litvin, Sean Smith, Caitlin Padgett, and Abbey Gibb: Each of you has had an indescribable impact on my life and business that can't be properly captured in an acknowledgments section. You have helped me become a more radically joy-full human who loves and trusts themself. You have also seen more in me than I did and believed in me when I didn't. I am honored to have *Joy-Full AF* contribute to your Ripples of Impact (ROI) in the world.

To my therapists, Sarah Rollins and Kayla LaJoie: I could not have asked for a better support team for managing my inner world and nervous system while writing a book, running a business, and having a personal life … all while living through a global pandemic. I am a more connected, curious, creative, courageous, compassionate, calm, clear, and confident person because of you.

To my 4PC and DFLA communities: What a merry band of travelers you have been for me over the last several years. My hero's journey would have been incomplete without you. Thank you for seeing, supporting, challenging, and inspiring me.

To the Wednesday Wonders, Jen Szad and Mahrukh Imtiaz: Thank goodness we decided all those years ago to ditch being a "goals mastermind" and become the tight-knit chosen family we are. Our friendships are some of my greatest joys. Thank you for the weekly deep conversations on all things personal development and business, but even more so, thank you for holding, cheerleading, and loving me.

To Laurie Shiers: There is no way this book would have seen the light of day without your unwavering belief in me and my writing. You epitomize joy and wonder. You inspire me to play, laugh, take life less seriously, and soak in being an amateur. And you remind me that taking time for a quick friend phone call during the middle of the workday is one of my not-so-secret pleasures.

To Allison Crow: My parts are grateful to have met and connected with such a kindred spirit during the pandemic and to have had you as a running buddy during the Garbage Post Challenge. Our mutual love of IFS, shared feelings about the coaching industry, and ability to hold space for one another's humanness has been lifeblood for me in this book process.

To my Kwan brothers, Matt Chavlovich and Andy Hite: You have kept my head on straight while also helping me keep the business running over the last two years. I'm deeply grateful for your support, love, and the occasional (okay, more than occasional) challenge of the stories I'm telling myself.

And finally, to Meryl Baker: I will forever be grateful for your mad editing skills. My book is more me thanks to you. But more so, I am thankful for your unflinching support and willingness to hold space when I needed to vent or melt down over these last two years. You have always encouraged me to follow my joy and have helped me re-find it when I've lost it.

About the Author

Dr. Erin Burgoon is a self-leadership coach, business strategist, social psychologist, Internal Family Systems practitioner, and official curator of joy. They hold a PhD from University of Texas at Austin and formerly held leadership roles at Facebook and Microsoft. Erin is known for their infectious energy, unapologetic authenticity, incisive wit, and unflinching commitment to helping their clients create joy-full AF businesses and lives that light them up.

The business world often recommends focusing on a singular audience, niche, or mission, but Erin realized early on that they have two equally important missions, and the most joy-full path has been to pursue both in their coaching, mentoring, teaching, and writing. First, they want to change the narrative in business about what truly creates impact and long-term success (putting joy front and center). Second, they want to create a more trauma-, neurodiversity-, mental health-, and systems-of-oppression-informed coaching industry.

Erin's clients are ambitious, values-driven, difference-makers who know the success and impact they crave hinges on them putting their joy first, but they're not quite sure how to get there on their own.

Beyond business, here are a few other things that fill Erin's joy tank:

- LGBTQIA+ and non-binary gender advocacy
- Collecting ties and bowties
- Rooting tirelessly for University of Michigan and University of Arizona sports — the size of their U of M gear collection rivals that of the tie collection
- Eccentric socks (especially ones with snarky phrases on them)
- Cuddling and playing with their tabby cat, Lou
- Playing golf
- Relearning classic rock solos from Pink Floyd on their guitar
- Climbing mountains and getting lost in the wilderness

To learn more about working with Erin, head over to https://drerinb.com or follow them on LinkedIn: https://www.linkedin.com/in/drerinb/.

www.ingramcontent.com/pod-product-compliance
Lightning Source LLC
Chambersburg PA
CBHW070138100426
42743CB00013B/2746